The Persuasive Project Manager: Communicating for Understanding

Dr. Bill Brantley, PMP, PMI-ACP

ISBN-13: 9781795728492

BOTTOM-LINE UP-FRONT

• This book helps you, the project manager, become a more effective and persuasive communicator so you can increase the chances for your project to succeed.

• Effective project management communication is when you and your audience co-create understanding from your communication. Meaning emerges from you and your audience exchanging messages—coordinated management of meaning.

• Understanding combines know-what, know-how, and know-why. The communicator must determine the desired amounts of know-what, know-how, and know-why needs to be in his or her message.

• Ninety percent of a project manager's work is communication. Much of that communication is in being persuasive. To be an effective persuader, a project manager must have credibility and trust (ethos). The project manager's message must have both logical arguments (logos) and an emotional impact (pathos).

• Project managers are the information hubs of the project. The number of communication channels on a project exponentially increases when you add team members. On a four-person project team, adding one more person increases the number of communication channels from six to 10. On a nine-person project team, adding another person increases the number of communication channels from 36 to 45. Think of communication channels as radio stations and you can see how overwhelmed project managers can be. Project managers need good communication governance processes.

• To be an effective communicator, project managers should be emotionally intelligent and culturally intelligent. Project managers should know how cognitive biases affect decision making.

• Project managers must understand how to build trust with remote workers and work around the communication barriers caused by online technologies.

• Project managers are increasingly using situational leadership, servant leadership, and coaching to help him or her lead project teams more effectively. At the heart of situational leadership, servant leadership, and coaching is creating understanding through communication.

TABLE OF CONTENTS

THE PERSUASIVE PROJECT MANAGER

CHAPTER ONE - UNDERSTANDING IS THE PURPOSE OF COMMUNICATION

As a practicing project manager, I have been on several projects that failed or were only partially successful because of poor communication. And I have been on many successful projects where the communication between the project manager, the project team, and the stakeholders was excellent. I am sure that you, whether you are a project manager or not, have noticed the communication difference in successful projects and unsuccessful projects.

The project goals were aligned with the project customer's expectations. The project vision was communicated by the project manager. Project team members seemed to read each other's minds as worked together on tasks. Stakeholders were happy and enthusiastic at every project status meeting. When things clicked together on a successful project, communication flows effortlessly, and no misunderstandings.

According to research from the Project Management Institute, "US$135 million is at risk for every US$1 billion spent on a project. **Further research on the importance of effective communications uncovers that a startling 56 percent (US$75 million of that US$135 million) is at risk due to ineffective communications** [emphasis in original].[i]

Five years later, the risk of poor communication in projects is still significant today according to CoreWorx,[ii] "[i]neffective communications is the primary contributor to project failure one-third of the time and had a negative impact on project success more than half the time."

Management researchers agree there is a direct link between project success and good communication:

"In terms of project success, communication has been strongly linked with project outcomes. Project team effectiveness and project performance depend on the degree and quality of communication between managers from different functional departments when cross-functional cooperation is required. Communication of project objectives and effective information are strongly related to project team performance. In addition, the aspects of communication (such as open discussion of diverse perspectives and participative communication processes) are positively associated with customer ratings of project performance. Enhancing clear communication channel and flow is one critical factor influencing project success and outcomes."[iii]

"What is good project management communication?" is a question I have been asking ever since I first learned about project management.

Why I Wrote This Book

In my study of what makes good project management communication, I discovered something important early on. Even though it is widely recognized how important communication is in project management, project management practitioners are not taking advantage of the latest findings in communication research. Project management communication, mostly, is still stuck in the outmoded information transfer model (sometimes called the "Shannon-Weaver Model" or the "transmission model") which doesn't work with today's complex and agile projects.

Simply put: communication theory and research have surpassed the project management communication model you and I, as project managers, have been taught. Now there are exceptions. I am sure that you have heard about successful projects that use excellent communication methods. In my research, I believe that I have discovered some tools and theories that make project management communication effective.

This book was written to show how new communication research can help revitalize project management communication for the new era of projects. First, I will give you a quick background about my quest.

My Life Long Quest to Understand Communication

As an undergraduate, I double-majored in speech communication and paralegal science. Paralegal science because I wanted a job when I graduated. Communication was my true passion. I was active on the speech team in high and enjoyed success as a college debater. My favorite classes were communication theory from the small group communication to organizational communication. Even after I graduated, I continued studying communication. In 1996, I obtained a master's in political management (essentially applied communication).

I worked a few political campaigns. In 1997, I won a Presidential Management Fellowship. The Presidential Management Fellowship is a two-year program where I would work as a management intern in a federal government agency. During the two years of the fellowship, I became heavily involved in project management and obtained an MBA in Project Management when I completed the fellowship in 1999.

Between 1997 and 2003, I became heavily involved with the rapidly-growing commercial Internet revolution. I worked on several Internet initiatives in the federal government. Starting in 2000, I worked for several Internet consulting companies while working on MBA in project management. Along with my project management courses, I took several marketing courses which taught me about copywriting and crafting persuasive messages.

In 2003, I had passed the Project Management Professional (PMP) certification exam having worked as an IT project manager for several years. I remember spending three months studying for the exam and even wrote an Amazon.com guide for other prospective PMP candidates. In 2003, there were only nine project management areas to master including project scope management, project budget management, and so on. When I came to the project communication management knowledge area, I was struck by how outdated project management communication theory was.

As PMPs know, the PMI's Project Management Book of

4

Knowledge (PMBOK) is a collection of the best practices for project management. Project managers from around the world are invited to submit project management methods, tools, and techniques for the latest edition of the PMBOK. Having participated in submitting ideas for subsequent revisions of the PMBOK, I think I am justified in stating that theory in the project communication management knowledge area represents the consensus of most project managers on what is good project management communication. And that is the problem.

I realize this is a bold statement and I hope that the rest of this book will justify my argument.

As a practicing project manager, I found that my communication skills as a college debater and my MBA marketing classes helped me lead successful projects. Thanks to my college debating experiencing and my marketing skills, I could master the soft skills of team-building, coaching, negotiation, and presentations. I became active in the Kentuckiana PMI chapter and started working on my Ph.D. in Public Policy and Management. During this time, I trained MBA students and local corporations in project management. Throughout that time, I supplemented the communication theory in the Project Management Body of Knowledge (PMBOK) with the latest communication methods and techniques.

I returned to Washington, D.C. to work in the federal government in 2008. In 2009, I completed my dissertation on communicating change visions in government projects which further deepened my interest in communication theory in project management. The usual practice for a newly-minted doctor is to turn their dissertation into an academic article or book. I started to but then thought that a better article would be an argument for applying modern communication theory to project management communication.

I have been to several project management conferences where practitioners spoke about their experiences using modern communication theory to manage their projects. However, much of the academic research on project management communication theory was still using a classic model of communication ("Shannon-Weaver Model") created in the late 1940s. While modern communication theory had taken the turn toward the "emergent" form of communication in which the participants co-created meaning through communication, project management communication theory was still stuck in the information transfer model.

Five Years of Research into Project Management Communication

In the early spring of 2013, I collected as many academic articles on project management communication as I could from the business and management journals. After some weeding out of duplicate articles and articles that were not research articles, I came up with 272 articles. Then, I placed the articles into four categories.

• Category 0 is where the articles only mentioned communication once or twice but no research about communication.

• Category 1 is where the articles used the information transfer model of communication but offered no new research on project management communication. These articles replicated previous research on the information transfer model.

• Category 2 did have new research about project management communication while using the information transfer model of communication as the basis for research. For example, an article may apply social network analysis to a project to determine how social networks may affect the transfer of information.

• Category 3 offered new research on project management communication that featured other communication frameworks rather than the information transfer model.

The purpose of the categories was to determine if project management communication has changed since the earliest research in the 1970s to research in 2016 (the latest revision of the article). Eighty-four percent of the 272 articles fell into Categories 0 or 1. Only 12% of the articles fit into Category 2. Four percent of articles fell into Category 3.

Category	Number of Articles	Percentage of Total Articles
0	117	43%
1	112	41%
2	33	12%
3	10	4%

Another interesting trend I found is that the bulk of the Category 2 and Category 3 articles indicated that intense research into project management communication began in the 1990s. Before the 1990s, the information transfer model was accepted as a given, and there was little research questioning that assumption.

Research into project management that didn't rely on the information transfer model began in the mid-2000s. An influential project management researcher is Koskinen who, in a 2013 article[iv], advocated for transitioning from the information transfer model to the "emergent communication" model. The emergent communication model is also known as the "Luhmann model" because it was a German sociologist, Niklas Luhmann, who first proposed the model.

I will explain Luhmann's model in more detail in chapter two but, the key feature of the emergent communication model is "understanding." Koskinen explains that bringing in understanding will help project managers become more effective in their communications. Koskinen's observations inspired my research on understanding. Koskinen validated my belief that creating understanding made me a more effective project manager.

What You Will Learn In the Coming Chapters:

• Chapter two is where I lay out the argument for why project management communication is more than information transfer. I explain the origins of the two competing communication theories and then make the argument of why understanding is essential to good communication.

• In chapter three, we examine Aristotle's classic persuasive triad of ethos, pathos, and logos. I demonstrate how ethos, pathos, and logos fit in well with three aspects of understanding I describe in chapter two.

• Chapter four is an introduction to a practical application of the emergent communication model called the "coordinated management of meaning" (CMM). CMM has been practiced by thousands of consultants since CMM's creation by Dr. Pearce in the mid-1970s. In this chapter, I will walk you through CMM tools to help you increase understanding in the communication between project team members and stakeholders.

• We revisit the information transfer model in chapter five as we explore the vital role of project managers as information hubs. I explain the importance of constructing effective information flows especially for large projects. Then, we will explore the use of storytelling in risk management to help promote clear communication and understanding.

• Chapter six is where we explore the importance of being emotionally-intelligent and culturally-intelligent in project management communication. I explain some emotional-intelligence and cultural-intelligence tools to help increase understanding in our communication.

• Closely-related to cultural-intelligence and emotional intelligence is how cognitive biases affect project management communication. In chapter seven, I discuss a tool for overcoming cognitive biases. I then discuss my general organizational failure model which demonstrates how the cognitive biases of decision makers and organizational teams lead to organizational failure.

• Chapter eight deals with communicating effectively with remote project team members and stakeholders. More project work is being performed online by distributed project teams. In this chapter, we explore how online communication affects understanding and ways to overcome the challenges of online communication.

• In chapter nine, I demonstrate how the emergent communication model is the foundation of situational leadership, servant leadership, and coaching. Project managers are increasingly encouraged to adopt these leadership styles because these leadership styles are good for engaging project team members. Project managers that use the emergent communication model will be more effective situational, servant, and coaching leaders.

• Chapter ten summarizes what we've learned and gives you practical steps on using the emergent communication model in your project management work.

I will expose you to some communication theory which, I think you will find interesting. But, as a practicing project manager, I realize you need more than theory. You will also read about practical tools and techniques to help you become a better communicator and manage your projects more effectively. There is a lot of good lessons from academic research and just as many good lessons from project management practitioners. I hope this book helps bridge the project management academic and practitioner worlds.

CHAPTER TWO - COMMUNICATION IS MORE THAN TRANSFERRING INFORMATION

One of my favorite phrases in class is to tell the students, "if you get nothing else out of this lecture, please remember this." So, if you get nothing else out of this book, please remember this:

Project management communication is more than just transferring information. Effective project management is creating understanding among the project manager, project team, and stakeholders.

To appreciate why understanding is so important, let me introduce two theories of communication and then explain what I mean by understanding.

The Shannon-Weaver Model of Communication (Information Transfer)

Claude Shannon[v] was a Bell Labs researcher who did pioneering work in improving the telephone network. His major contribution was the creation of the Shannon-Weaver Model of Communication. This model is still a part of the PMBOK's section on project communication management. You probably have seen this model often in communication training.

There are several variations on the model, but the major components are essentially the same. First, the sender creates a message through encoding. The message is transmitted via a channel to a receiver who decodes the message. Here is an example to illustrate how the model works.

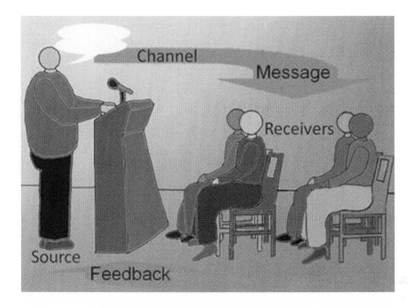

Figure 1: Information Transfer Model of Communication

Imagine you are making a phone call. You speak into the phone which turns your vocalizations into electrical impulses transmitted over the cellular phone network. When the electrical impulses are transmitted to the cell phone you want to call, the electrical impulses are then turned into sounds that come from the cell phone's speaker.

Now, anyone who has made a phone call knows that sometimes static comes into the call. This interference with your phone call is what Shannon called "noise in the channel." His breakthrough insight was to decrease the noise in the channel. The technical term for the information lost to noise is "entropy." Shannon developed a set of equations to increase the information that can be transmitted in a channel. Reducing entropy evolved from a purely technical topic to the communication practice of clearly transmitting information by becoming a better speaker and writer.

Clearly transmitting messages is a good communication practice but, taken to the extreme, precludes effective communication. If the communicator believes that communicating a clear message is enough for good communication, then the communicator may be fooled into believing his or her communication efforts are complete.

Even if there is feedback, the feedback is usually limited to confirming that the message was received as intended. The focus on transmitting information is why the Shannon-Weaver model is also called the information transfer model of communication.

As a practicing project manager, I knew that just merely telling my team, stakeholders, and executive sponsor information did not mean I was communicating effectively. Yes, I was technically communicating but just giving information didn't mean I was an effective communicator. What was needed is another component added to the transmission communication model – understanding.

The Luhmann Model of Communication (Emergence)

Fifteen years earlier, a famous German sociologist, Niklas Luhmann[vi], created his theory of communication. Much like the transmission model of communication, Luhmann's theory had senders and receivers who exchanged messages. Luhmann called the messages "information" and the process of sending messages as "utterances." To information and utterances, Luhmann added the act of "understanding." Understanding implies the encoding and decoding of messages but also includes the feedback loop by which the sender and receiver co-create meaning from the communication.

Admittedly, this is a simplified explanation of Luhmann's theory of communication. In Luhmann's theory, the participants work together to create meaning during the communication process. As he would say, understanding also could mean misunderstanding because the information being transmitted doesn't necessarily imply the same information is received. People will interpret the information and utterances based on their knowledge and opinions.

Let me illustrate with a classic story.

You may have heard of a ship's captain steaming back into port. As the ship approaches the port, the captain spots a bright light which seems to head right for the ship.

"Please alter course by 15 degrees starboard," transmits the captain over the radio.

"Request that you alter course by 15 degrees port," is the reply.

The captain, becoming irritated, repeats his command. Again, the reply is for the captain to alter his course instead.

"I am the captain of a U.S. Navy battleship, and I have priority for that port. You must immediately alter your course to allow my ship to dock!" demands the captain.

There is a moment of silence, and then the captain hears someone clear their voice over the radio. "Uh, captain, I can't alter course. I'm in a lighthouse."

As seen in the story, both parties were transmitting information but, it wasn't until the captain understood the context of lighthouse keeper that understanding can begin. The rest of this book uses the Luhmann Communication Triad as the context for becoming a better communicator. But, before I explain the practical application of Luhmann's Communication Triad, let me define understanding.

What is Understanding?

Understanding is a topic in epistemology which is the study of knowledge. Don't worry; I will keep the philosophy brief and to the point. Even though the study of knowledge is ancient, the study of understanding is relatively new (just like the study of project management communication). According to philosophers, there three main ways of understanding.

There is *know-what* in which I have an understanding of some concept, physical object, or process. For example, I know what a work-breakdown-structure (WBS)[vii] is in the sense of it being a tool in project management. I may have a simple understanding of what a WBS is because I recognize a WBS when I see it. Or my know-what may be that I know WBS exist but, that is all I know. In contrast, I may thoroughly understand WBS including the history of the concept. Know-what is often the first step in creating understanding.

When I can construct a WBS, I have *know-how*. As you can see, know-how is more involved than know-what. For me to have know-how, I must possess these six attributes:

1. Ability to follow the explanation of the concept, physical object, or process.

2. Ability to explain the concept, physical object, or process.

3. Ability to draw conclusions from the concept, physical object, or process.

4. Ability to conclude opposing conclusions from the opposite of the concept, physical object, or process.

5. Ability to conclude the correct ideas when given the concept, physical object, or process.

6. Ability to conclude the correct opposite ideas when given the opposite of the concept, physical object, or process.

The third way of understanding is *know-why*. You may know what a WBS is and how to construct the WBS. However, your understanding is incomplete if you don't know why you need to use a WBS. Know-why may seem the same as know-what, but there is a significant difference. For example, I may be an expert on Monte Carlo[viii] simulations in risk management. I can explain the concept and even create a spreadsheet that uses Monte Carlo simulations for risk management. However, I may not be able to explain why you need a Monte Carlo simulation in your project. I just want to use a Monte Carlo simulation in your simple weekend project to build a deck just because I like building Monte Carlo simulations. I know-what and I know-how but I don't know-why we shouldn't use the Monte Carlo simulation in your particular project.

It is unnecessary to have three ways of understanding to be effective. For example, your senior sponsor may only need to know why your project needs a risk register but, has only a partial understanding of what a risk register is. The senior sponsor doesn't need to understand how to create a risk register. And the senior sponsor needs only a cursory understanding of why a risk register is needed. Just enough know-what and know-why to reassure the sponsor that the project's chances for success will increase if you use a risk register.

An important decision for a communicator is to determine the level of understanding that his or her audience needs for successful communication. That is why communication is more than information transfer. The communicator and the receiver must use feedback to determine how the message was received and if the communicator created the intended level of understanding in the receiver for the communication to succeed.

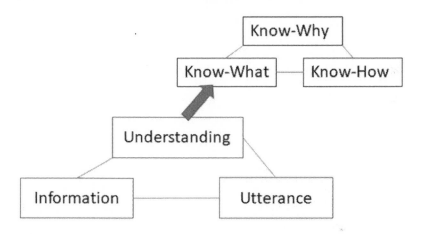

Figure 2: The Emergence Communication Model with the Understanding Triangle

Lessons Learned for the Project Manager

• Two major models of communication apply to project management communication.

• The first model is the information transfer model which focuses on the clear transmission of messages between senders and receivers. The goal is to reduce the noise in the channel which can affect the transmission of messages.

• The second model is the emergence model. The emergence model closely resembles the information transfer model because it also deals with the transmission of information.

• The difference between the two models is that the emergence model has a third component of understanding.

• Understanding comprises three components: know-what, know-how, and know-why. These three components can be of varying proportions for understanding to take place.

• When project managers create communications, he or she should work to ensure that the message is transmitted clearly and for the desired level of understanding on the part of the receivers.

CHAPTER 3 - ETHOS, PATHOS, AND LOGOS

Aristotle[ix], the ancient Greek philosopher, and tutor to Alexander the Great, was a master of persuasion. His three elements for being persuasive still applies after 2000 years of history. You had probably heard of ethos, pathos, and logos when you had a high school or college class on giving speeches. Have you ever wondered what makes these three elements so effective? Are ethos, pathos, and logos still relevant for project managers who work with multiple team members that may be distributed around the world?

In the next three sections, I will demonstrate why ethos, pathos, and logos are still the foundation for being persuasive.

Ethos

Ethos is loosely translated from the original Greek as the speaker's credibility and stage presence. When discussing ethos with my students, I emphasize that the more ethos a speaker is perceived to have, the more the audience will believe what the speaker says. In explaining how ethos helps a project manager be persuasive, the students and I explore the bases of power.

French and Raven first established the five bases of power to which they added the sixth base in 1974. These six bases are coercive, rewards, legitimate, referent, expert, and informational. Project managers will have legitimate power by being appointed as project manager. However, legitimate power is then replaced by referent power and expert power as the project team, and stakeholders feel part of the project and rely on the project manager's expertise to deliver the project.

Therefore, the project manager's ethos rests upon how well he or she demonstrates his or her expertise while constantly encouraging a feeling of belonging to the project. Think of how famous project managers such as John Kelly of Lockheed's Skunkworks or Werner von Braun of the Saturn Five rocket used both their expertise and ability to enlist people into the project vision. That is the project manager's ethos.

Roger Ailes, advisor to President Reagan and founder of FOX News, and Alan Alda, famous actor and author, have both written about the importance of ethos in being persuasive. Ailes famously told President Reagan that "you are the message" in how President Reagan's stage presence established his credibility as President. Alda's book, *If I Understood You, Would I Have This Look on My Face,* explains how to develop ways of expressing your credibility so audiences will be more willing to accept what you said.

However, ethos is more than just demonstrating expertise. Ethos is about people's trust in your word. As Judith Glaser writes in *Conversational Intelligence,*

Conversations are not what we think they are. We've grown up with a narrow view of conversations, thinking they are about talking, sharing information, telling people what to do, or telling others what's on our minds. We are now learning, through neurological and cognitive research, that a "conversation" goes deeper and is more robust than simple information sharing. Conversations are dynamic, interactive, and inclusive. They evolve and impact the way we connect, engage, interact, and influence others, enabling us to shape reality, mind-sets, events, and outcomes in a collaborative way. Conversations have the power to move us from "power over" others to "power with" others, giving us the exquisite ability to get on the same page with our fellow humans and experience the same reality by bridging the reality gaps between "how you see things and how I see things." (from the "Introduction")

To understand Ms. Glaser's conversational intelligence model, let me introduce another important concept. According to the Nobel Prize winner in economics, Daniel Kahneman, there are two systems of thinking. *System 1* is our fast, often unconscious, and emotional way of reacting to events in our world. *System 2* is the slower more deliberate way of thinking in which we consciously consider our decisions. You may have had the experience where you are listening to someone saying all the right things, but you have a feeling that the person is just dishonest. Your feeling is distrust comes from when you System 1 thinking is competing with your System 2 thinking.

Ms. Glaser then describes how trust and distrust live in two different parts of our brain. Trust is found in the prefrontal cortex of our brain which is the center of System 2 thinking. Mostly, people are slow to trust and need time to test if the person is worthy of trust. But it takes less than a second to distrust. That is because distrust is centered in the person's amygdala. Primarily the amygdala protects us from threats – especially things (or people) we can't trust. Your System 1 thinking probably has lots of rules-of-thumb for distrust. Sometimes, these rules-of-thumb are unfortunate prejudices based on stereotypes which takes much work on the System 2 side to overcome.

To help understand where one is regarding conversational intelligence, Ms. Glaser created the *Conversational Dashboard*. The dashboard is divided into three levels which describe the journey from distrust to trust. In level one, we are dominated by the amygdala which protects us by resisting and being skeptical of the communication. Level one is the "tell – ask" level of communication. The second level is the "advocate – inquire" level of communication in which we are between the amygdala and the prefrontal cortex as we take a "wait and see" attitude in the conversation. The third level is where our prefrontal cortex is fully engaged, and we partner with the other person in the conversation. We are experimental and work to co-create meaning in conversations. We are in the trust stage of communication.

Good Communication Builds Trust

Before discussing the other two parts of Aristotle's persuasion triangle, let's examine how good communication helps the communicator build trust with his audience. David Horsager writes about the eight pillars of trust in his book, *The Trust Edge: How Top Leaders Gain Faster Results, Deeper Relationships, and a Stronger Bottom Line.* When you read through the eight pillars, you can see how communication plays a role in each pillar.

Pillar 1: Clarity - People trust the clear and mistrust the ambiguous.

Pillar 2: Compassion - People put faith in those who care beyond themselves.

Pillar 3: Character - People notice those who do what is right over what is easy.

Pillar 4: Competency - People have confidence in those who stay fresh, relevant, and capable.

Pillar 5: Commitment - People believe in those who stand through adversity.

Pillar 6: Connection - People want to follow, buy from, and be around friends.

Pillar 7: Contribution - People immediately respond to results.

Pillar 8: Consistency - People love to see the little things done consistently.

Let's focus on the first pillar, clarity. Horsager writes: "People in organizations typically spend over 75 percent of their time in interpersonal situations; thus it is no surprise to find that at the root of a large number of organizational problems is poor communication." He further notes that "[s] ocial psychologists estimate that there is usually a 40%–60% loss of meaning in the transmission of messages from sender to receiver." Horsager echoes the message of this book in that "communication is shared meaning." Even though we cannot communicate perfectly, Horsager argues that the clearer a leader communicates, the more likely people will trust that leader.

In 2012, Google started Project Aristotle to study what made a high-performing team. The researchers first tried to determine if it was the people that composed the teams. Team composition did not seem to matter. The researchers did more analysis and discovered that group norms played a major role. "The right norms, in other words, could raise a group's collective intelligence, whereas the wrong norms could hobble a team, even if, individually, all the members were exceptionally bright."

Delving deeper into the group norms, researchers found two behaviors consistent to all good groups. The first behavior is that the group members "spoke in roughly the same proportion, a phenomenon the researchers referred to as 'equality in distribution of conversational turn taking.'" The second behavior is that the good teams had "high 'average social sensitivity' – a fancy way of saying they were skilled at intuiting how others felt based on their tone of voice, their expressions, and other nonverbal cues." These two behaviors make up *psychological safety* in which team members trust each and have mutual respect. Team members feel safe to be themselves and take risks.

An important part of psychological safety is communication – communication that creates understanding. Look how the first behavior encourages equal give and take between group members. Couple that with the second behavior in which team members closely observe each other to see the reactions to each of their communications. Team members create psychological safety so that understanding can flourish between them. Trust is both the foundation and result of understanding because it helps meaning to emerge in our communication.

Pathos

Pathos is the emotional part of the persuasive message. It does not matter how technical and dry your subject is; to be persuasive, you must have an emotional impact on the message to be persuasive. That is because of how we process information and think about our world. Emotions are so powerful because of a special part of our brain's structure and one of the two systems of thinking.

Deep inside your brain is the amygdala which constantly scans information from your senses looking for threats. If you have been in a tense situation where you feel like you couldn't think or had a strong reaction, that is your amygdala taking control of your brain – the amygdala hijack. You also know the amygdala as the "fight, flee, or freeze" response. The amygdala hijack is also why you have stage fright as you may feel threatened by being the center of attention when you stand up to speak.

As well as helping you to respond to threats, the amygdala is also important in forming long-term memories. During a typical day, you receive millions of bits of information from your senses. Much of that information is forgotten as the information travels from your senses to your short-term memory. That is a good thing because most of your sensory information is trivial and not worth remembering (such as what you had for lunch or the number of people you passed on your morning walk to work).

However, sometimes, you need to remember something because of its importance to you. The hippocampus is the brain structure that transfers selected memories from your short-term memory to your long-term memory. The amygdala sits on top of the hippocampus and provides an emotional tag to the memory being transferred from the short-term memory to the long-term memory.

Now, the emotional tag need not be overwhelmingly emotional. It is just enough that the emotion is enough to signify that the memory is important to keep. For example, you may find a new lunch place with an exceptional menu. Your feelings of pleasure from a good lunch is enough for you to put that memory of the restaurant in your long-term memory.

For you to be effective as a persuader, you must attend to the emotional aspects of your message because you want your important points to be remembered and to have both thinking systems working with each other.

Logos

Now we come to what most people think makes a message persuasive. Presenting logical and rational arguments is important. I'm sure you have the experience of listening to a person who seems credible and presents an emotionally-compelling speech. But, when you consider his or her words later, you realize there wasn't much substance to the message. Essentially, the persuader gave you all sizzle and no steak.

As the amygdala is associated with pathos, the cerebral cortex is associated with logos. In brain anatomy, the cerebral cortex is a more recently evolved structure in the human brain. It plans and makes decisions – the project manager of your brain if you will. System 2 thinking is also closely associated with your cerebral cortex. Ethos and pathos help you to gain your audience's attention and engagement with your message. But it is logos that persuades your audience.

Ethos, Pathos, and Logos Meets Information, Utterances, and Understanding

In chapter 2, I discussed why Luhmann's Communication Triad is a good model for effective persuasive communication. Ethos, Pathos, and Logos further reinforce the value of Luhmann's Communication Triad – especially understanding.

By creating a balance between ethos, pathos, and logos, the persuader creates a message that grabs the attention of the audience that then engages people with a balance of emotional impact and logical arguments. A person doesn't understand when they are not paying attention, is not engaged with the speaker, and doesn't remember what was said. Ethos, pathos, and logos also aid the speaker by helping in the selection of information to present and how to fashion the utterances for the best effect.

In the next chapter, we will take a deeper dive into creating understanding with our project teams and stakeholders. The key is to create *coordinated management of meaning* as we take the *communicative approach* to understand our audience's different *social worlds*. The purpose of coordinated management meaning is to break out of a vicious cycle of miscommunication to create understanding among people.

Lessons Learned for the Project Manager

• Ethos, pathos, and logos are an ancient concept of persuasion still relevant for today's communicators.

• Ethos (credibility) and pathos (emotions) are linked to the emotional center of the brain – the amygdala.

• Logos (logic) is linked to the intellectual center of the brain – the prefrontal cortex.

• Ethos and pathos also rely on System 1 of our thinking processes because we rely on our unconscious impressions and rules-of-thumb to quickly draw conclusions about communicators.

• Logos relies on System 2 which can be more influential but requires more time and mental energy on behalf of the audience.

• Trust and distrust are in two different parts of the brain. Distrust works faster and is harder to overcome because the amygdala determines what we distrust based on the perception of potential threat. Trust is in the prefrontal cortex and requires time and significant evidence to overcome the influence of the amygdala.

• The emergent model of communication with the understanding triangle complements the ethos, pathos, and logos triangle.

CHAPTER FOUR - COMMUNICATION CONSTITUTES PROJECT: THE COORDINATED MANAGEMENT OF MEANING IN PROJECTS

This chapter is the core of the book because it expands on the emergence model of communication by describing how to create understanding between communicators. I will describe an approach to communication that recognizes that each us live in several *social worlds* simultaneously. Recognizing and understanding each other's social worlds is the key to effective communication.

The best way to understand what a social world is to think of the number of social worlds you inhabit. There is the social world of being a project manager in which assume the role of a project manager where you take expected actions and react in predictable ways with project team members and stakeholders. Then, there is the social world of being part of a family where you may assume the role of a father, mother, brother, sister, aunt, or uncle. For each role in the family social world, you interact with other family members in anticipated ways. Then, there is the social world of your religious beliefs, political beliefs, and so on. In each social world, you inhabit a role and perform interactions appropriate to that role.

The creator of the social world's concept, Dr. W. Barnett Pearce, writes: "Our social worlds are made in the dance between the two faces of the communication process: coordinating actions and making/managing meaning. This is the site where speech acts, episodes and forms of communication, selves and forms of consciousness, and relationships and minds are made."[x]

Realizing that communication takes place when social worlds meet, Dr. Pearce created the *coordinated management of meaning* theory in the 1970s. As he describes the moment, he was assigned to teach a class in communication. He decided that he wanted to take a new approach to teach communication by basing his new approach to "taking the communication perspective." That meant stepping outside of a communication event and observing how participants created meaning by coordinating actions.

Dr. Pearce realized that teaching just the transmission (information transfer) perspective of communication would be incomplete. Incomplete because of the main assumption of the transmission perspective – perfect correspondence between what is communicated and what is understood. The transmission model either ignores the concept of social worlds or presupposes that the communicators share the same social world with a perfect understanding of each other's perspectives. If miscommunication occurs, it is because the message wasn't clear, the channel was low-fidelity, or there is an interpretation problem. If the message is properly encoded, transmitted, and received, then understanding must occur – according to the transmission perspective.

However, we all have encountered situations where the message was formed, sent, and received successfully but, understanding did not occur. How often have you created a project plan or communicated a risk event you knew was fully communicated and received but did not trigger the required actions on behalf of the recipient? It wasn't a problem with the message but how the communication fit into the recipient's social world. Or maybe your social world influenced your perspective of the message you transmitted.

In taking the communication perspective, Dr. Pearce suggests asking three questions. What are we making together? How are we making it? And how can we make better social worlds?

Dr. Pearce's theory illustrates that meaning emerges from how each person in the communication event respond to and transmit messages. And meaning is still being actively created even after the communication event is over. How often have you replayed in your head at bedtime, the conversations you have had during the day?

Enough theory. How does the coordinated management of meaning work in a practical sense? Over the years, CMM practitioners have created methods and tools to make the communication perspective visible. We will examine one tool to aid you in taking the communication perspective.

A Communication Perspective Example

SEAVA is an acronym for **S**toryboarding, **E**nriching, **A**nalyzing what holds the pattern together, **V**isioning preferred alternative patterns, and **A**cting intentionally. We will go through each part of the SEAVA tool to demonstrate how to make the communication perspective visible.

Storyboarding – In this process, the CMM consultant questions the participants in a crisis to understand how their communications and actions led to the crisis. The first part is to identify the key episode that led to the crisis. Then, working forward and backward from the key episode, the CMM consultant and participants storyboard the communications and actions around the key event. The purpose is to determine the communication pattern that led to the key episode.

Let's say you are a project manager of a ten-person project team. You are to put on a three-day training event for 500 managers flown in from all the world for this event. You must create the training schedule, securing the speakers, and the logistics of the event. Everything is going as planned except, two months before the event; two team members come to you ready to quit because they can't get along with each other. These two members are key to your logistics.

You call the two team members into your office to storyboard the problem. The key episode is when one team member called the office that handles the room arrangements at the facility for the training event. He told the facility office to ignore previous room arrangements for the conference in favor of new arrangements he was sent to the facility office. When the other team member later called the facility office, she was incensed to hear that her room arrangements had been discarded.

Working from this key episode, you learn that the two members were never clear about their role and responsibilities for the training logistics. They initially had an informal agreement about who would do what but, as events overtook them, they never revisited the agreement and both, admittedly, decided without consulting each other because there "wasn't just enough time." Communication that started as face-to-face became emails and then dwindled to no communication. Each person made decisions without consulting the other person.

You capture this communication sequence on a whiteboard with the key episode in the middle and the events leading up to the communication breakdown on the left. After the key episode, you work with the participants to diagram the consequences of the key episode. The purpose is to determine the communication turns that each participant took in response to the other participant.

Enriching – Once the CMM consultant and participants are satisfied that the communication pattern has been completely described, two more tools are used to understand the participants' social worlds. The first approach is to use *LUUUTT* which stands for:

- stories **L**ived

- **U**ntold stories

- **U**nheard stories

- **U**nknown stories

- **U**ntellable stories

- stories **T**old

- story**T**elling

Surrounding the communications and interactions of the key episode are the stories that make up each participant's social worlds.

Going back to our story of the training event, you take the participants through their stories. The female team member sees this assignment as her way to step-up, and she wants to make a good impression on you and the senior sponsor so you will feel confident in giving her bigger projects. The male team member is younger and chafing under the Millennial stereotype that others on the project team pin on him. He wants to prove that he is mature and capable of greater responsibility and sees this project as a way to prove himself.

After identifying the LUUUUTTs, the CM consultant uses the Daisy Model to understand each participant's social circle. Even though some of the social circle's participants may not be present during the communication event, their influence can affect how the participant communicates and interacts. Each participant lists the social worlds influencing their actions. For example, the male team member may list his work colleagues, his parents, and friends outside of work. These are the people that the male team member wants to impress or asks for advice. The female team member also lists her social worlds in the Daisy Model.

When the participants in our training example create their Daisy Model, they are surprised by how much in common their social circles are. They realize that part of their motivation is to look good to their social circles, so they inadvertently created a zero-sum contest between themselves.

Analyzing – After the LUUUUTT stories are identified, the participants rank the stories in a hierarchy to understand how the stories influence the participant's actions. After ranking the stories, the participants determine the *logical forces* that compelled their actions. The logical actions are ranked in order of "shouldness" from 1 to 5. The object is to determine what stories are being used to motivate the participants.

The logical forces that compelled our participants in the training event example were easy to identify and rank. The first logical force was to use this training event as a way to move up. The second logical force was to prove their selves as project managers to gain the confidence of their superiors. And the third logical force was to build their legacy. Again, both team members' same logical forces inevitably forced the conflict.

Visioning – At this point, the communication perspective should be clear to all participants with an understanding of what is motivating each participant. The participants then work together to determine the preferred communication patterns.

After diagnosing the communication problem between the two team members, you work with them to envision how they should communicate so both team members can achieve their goals. The two team members both agree that they negotiate the roles and responsibilities. The team members than agree to develop ways to keep each other informed about decisions and create a way to decide together.

Acting Intentionally – The participants identify how they can take actions to bring about the desired communication patterns. In the training event example, the team members agree to formalize the roles and responsibilities through written position descriptions. The team members also establish a formal method of consulting with each other on decisions while the project manager agrees to help formally recognize the contributions each project team member has made to the project.

By using the SEAVA tool, participants can walk through each other's social worlds and work to create a shared social world of understanding together. Although taking the communication perspective takes much more work and shouldn't be used in all communication situations where you only need to transfer information, you can see the value of created shared social worlds that help with subsequent project management communications.

Lessons Learned for the Project Manager

• Meaning emerges from our communication events and not just solely from the sender transferring information to the receiver.

• People inhabit several social worlds where they assume roles and interact with others based on that role in that social world.

• To communicate effectively, we need to take the communication perspective by asking these three questions: What meaning are we making together? How are we making this meaning together? How can we make better social worlds together through communication?

• The coordinated management of meaning theory gives us effective tools for taking the communication perspective such as

SEAVA: Storyboarding, Enriching, Analyzing, Visioning, and Acting intentionally

• We construct meaning from our communications before, during, and after communication events.

CHAPTER FIVE - PROJECT MANAGERS AS THE HUB IN PROJECT INFORMATION FLOWS

In the previous chapters, I wrote about the importance of understanding in project management communication. In this chapter, I want to switch gears and talk about the value of the information transfer model in project management communication. The power of Shannon-Weaver's information transfer theory is developing a framework creating clear communication. Even Luhmann's communication theory, which came over ten years earlier than Shannon-Weaver's theory recognizes the importance of clearly transmitting information in communication.

The value of information transfer is apparent in the many academic articles that study information transfer in project management. As I observed in the first chapter, most of the articles in my research were grounded in the information transfer model. Most of the academic articles recognized that project managers are the hub in project information flows. Practicing project managers can verify that most of their daily work is communication.

Being a Good Communicator is a Necessary Skill for Project Managers

"Being a good communicator as a project manager assures, in the end, the successful completion of the project (p. 1563)."[xi]

"In terms of project success, communication has been strongly linked with project outcomes. Project team effectiveness and project performance depend on the degree and quality of communication between managers from different functional departments when cross-functional cooperation is required. Communication of project objectives and effective information are strongly related to project team performance. In addition, the aspects of communication (such as open discussion of diverse perspectives and participative communication processes) are positively associated with customer ratings of project performance. Enhancing clear communication channel and flow is one critical factor influencing project success and outcomes (p. 54)."[xii]

"Literature advises project managers to be aware that project stakeholders rely on several communication channels, which includes not only face-to-face and written media, but also telephonic/verbal communication. Project managers on the other hand have a strong preference for verbal communication over other forms. These communication type preferences and the fact that the project or programme [sic] manager is at the centre [sic] of the project delivery process is a real communication management challenge. He or she must maintain a range of complex communication channels with different types of organisations [sic] while still facilitating and managing frequent communication with the project members and stakeholders, to ensure project success (p. 1009)."[xiii]

Communication Lessons from the Big Dig Project

In my project management class, I have the students read case studies on Boston's Big Dig. I use the Big Dig project as a good example of how important managing information and communication flows are in project management.

If you are unfamiliar with the particulars of the Big Dig project, here are the details.

• Officially known as the Central Artery/Tunnel Project (CA/T). The purpose was to reroute Interstate 93 into the Thomas P. O'Neill Jr. Tunnel, build the Ted Williams Tunnel, the Leonard P. Zakim Bunker Hill Memorial Bridge, and the Rose Kennedy Greenway.

• Construction began in 1991 and was scheduled to end in 1998. Construction actually ended in 2007.

• The original estimated cost was $2.8 billion (1982 dollars). The cost at completion was actually $14.6 billion ($8.08 billion in 1982 dollars). The cost overrun was 190%.

• From the beginning, the project was plagued with problems from badly-drawn design blueprints, engineering flaws, and construction problems.

• The most tragic event was the death of a woman struck by a falling ceiling panel as she traveled in a newly-opened tunnel.

Virginia Greiman, in her 2013 book, *Mega Project Management: Lessons on Risk and Project Management from the Big Dig*, lists these key lessons learned about stakeholder management from the Big Dig:

1. "Be proactive in the management of stakeholder expectations" (p. 101).

2. "Develop stakeholder partnerships" (p. 102).

3. "Communication is a two-way street" (p. 102).

4. "Build honesty and trust with your stakeholders" (p 102).

5. "Plan stakeholder management into your project budget" (p. 102).

6. "Acknowledge when mistakes are made and apologize for those mistakes" (p. 103).

7. "Use stakeholders to identify risk and opportunities" (p. 103).

8. "Reward stakeholders for their contributions" (p. 103).

As you can see from the eight key lessons, project managers are at the center for managing stakeholders through good communication management. The Big Dig example provides a cautionary tale when project management communication flows are not well-managed. Probably the most important lesson from the Big Dig is how quickly communication can become complex and convoluted in a project.

Communication Complexity

When working with students or training new project managers, I like to start with this equation when we discuss project management communication. It is a simple equation with profound implications. It is the equation for calculating the number of communication channels between a number of communication sources - number of communicators times number of communicators minus 1 divided by two or $n(n-1)/2$.

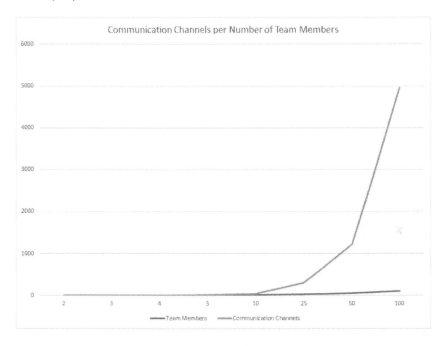

Figure 3: Communication Channels Equation

So, if we have two communicators, there is only one communication channel. Add a second communication channel, and you have three communication channels. Jump to the size of a small project team (around ten people) and the project manager now has 45 communication channels to monitor. If you imagine each communication channel as a radio station, you can see how quickly the project manager can be overwhelmed with all the information coming in.

On the Big Dig, there were 40 general contractors over 200 subcontractors. It is estimated that over 5,000 people were working on the project at the times of the most construction. That is nearly 12 and half million potential communication channels. Now, no single Big Dig project manager had to handle all 12.5 million communication channels. But, as you can imagine, there was a lot of information flowing among the contractors and subcontractors that needed to be managed effectively. [xiv]

However, as my students found, information was not being managed effectively. When I have my undergraduate engineering students discuss this case in class, they focus on in the engineering mistakes made. The wrong concrete being used for the structures. The roof bolts couldn't hold the weight of the roof tiles. Inadequate drainage for the underground tunnels. And with every example of an engineering mistake, I ask why weren't the concerns communicated early? Who oversaw the information and why didn't they stop these mistakes before they happened?

The number of communication channels is not the only reason that project management communication can become complex. As Stephen Leybourne, Vijay, Kanabar, and Roger Warburton explain in their 2010 paper, "Understanding and Overcoming Communications Complexity in Projects[xv]," communication complexity can arise from several factors:

1. The number of communication links.

2. Errors in transmitting messages.

3. Cultural differences.

4. The size of the project including a rapid increase in the number of project tasks and number or resources to manage.

5. The ability of the project manager to persuade people and deal with the politics of working with many people.

6. An inadequate project communication plan and an insufficient understanding of the project communication requirements.

The authors conclude their paper with these observations:

"Understanding the influence of complexity and ambiguity within the project domain is the key to effective project communication. Communications complexity can result in communications failure in large projects. At a theoretical level, the project manager must design team clusters with well-formed independent

boundaries to manage communications in a large project. Designing well-formed smaller sub-groups will reduce the communication efforts for all parties concerned and reduce the chances of project failure. In this paper we have also identified the fundamental key points that a project manager can adopt. For instance, creating a comprehensive communications management plan will go a long way in ensuring project success."

Risk Management as Communication Management

After talking about the Big Dig, I then go into my lecture about standard project management communication tools. I present templates that document who, when, where, what, and how project management information should be communicated. As I explain to my students and new project managers, it is vital to establish good communication practices in the planning stages of the project. Good practices such as establishing regular meetings with the executive sponsor, stakeholders, and the project team. Determining how to communicate project status regularly. Understanding how the stakeholders and project team want to receive information. All these practices are necessary and should be documented. However, there is a major project management practice that is, at its core, another manifestation of project communication management.

Project risk management is a widely-recognized vital part of project management. Good risk management is probably the single most important factor in project management success. I'm in awe of how well some risk management specialists can use their analytical methods to develop elaborate mathematical models for determining project risks and strategies for avoiding or controlling project risks. I think it is the very sophistication and expertise that prevents project risk management from being more effective. What is missing is seeing project risk management as another form of project communication management.

Think of how project managers determine project risks. First, you start with the project vision, project products, work breakdown structure, schedule, and resources list. Then, the project manager with the project team and stakeholders brainstorm possible project risk events. From the list of possible project risks, project managers and risk analysts determine the probability and impact of the risk event. For risks considered worth paying attention to, they are listed on the risk register. Then risk response strategies are created, and the risks are monitored.

So, given this well-known and commonly-understood process, why didn't the project managers and risk experts do a better job with risks on the Big Dig? Because there was no understanding due to the massive complexity of all the project information. Think back to the example of each communication channel being a radio station. How many communication channels/radio stations could a project manager monitor before becoming overwhelmed and missing information? I don't know the exact number, but I bet that even the 45 communication channels of a ten-person project team can quickly overwhelm the project manager.

In very few risk management plans, have I seen the risk of information overload. However, as the number of risk events accumulates on a project, where is the process for making sure the risks are being communicated to the right parties in time to handle the risks? What strategies are being used to reduce the details of the many risk events to a clear picture of the problems confronting the project?

Storytelling as Risk Management Communication

Human brains are naturally designed for stories. We have brain structures devoted to making sense of the world in cause-effect terms. Personally, one thing that I think is wrong with many project management conferences I go to is the admonishment for presenters not to fill up the time with war stories. For me, the most useful parts of the presentations are often the war stories – well told. A good project war story sets the context, tells me the problem, a possible solution, and how well the solution worked. Good stories are like flight simulators in that you can try out various approaches to a problem before tackling the real problem.

Think of the Big Dig example I have used in this chapter. The first case study I assign to the students is a news report about a woman killed by a falling roof tile when her family was driving through a newly-opened tunnel. I could have started with a list of problems with the Big Dig construction, an analysis of the number of communication channels, or a matter-of-fact chronology of the project. Starting with an emotionally impactful event sets the stage for understanding how poor communication management among the Big Dig contractors led to the engineering problems of the project.

When I was working on my dissertation, I used an approach to risk communication pioneered by M. Granger Morgan, Baruch Fischoff, Ann Bostrom, and Cynthia J. Atman. They advocate creating "mental models" about risks based on how experts perceive a specific risk event. The example they use in their book, *Risk Communication: A Mental Models Approach*, is how to create an effective public information campaign to warn the public about radon danger. Most members of the general public are not well-informed about what radon is and the dangers it poses.

In their research, Morgan, Fischoff, Bostrom, and Atman, interviewed experts on radon. From these interviews, the researchers created an expert mental model and then communicated this model to the general public. The expert mental model not only explained what radon was but also how to protect against radon exposure. The expert mental model is then used to create an evidence-based risk communication to help in better persuading the public about the radon risk. Their advice is especially useful to project managers: "Before disseminating a risk message, communicators must characterize expert knowledge about the risk, study current beliefs, examine the risk decisions that people face, develop a communication focused on critical content, and evaluate the message through empirical testing."[xvi]

Wrapping the expert mental model of the risk in a story is a good approach to gain people's attention and engage them long enough for the absorption of the expert mental model. As I wrote before, stories serve as flight simulators letting the listeners try out new ideas without actually implementing the new idea. Here, the listeners can simulate the risk event embedded in the expert mental model without being exposed to real risk.

Thus, the lessons of this chapter are threefold. One, the imperatives of the information transfer model to build clear channels for communicating information is vital to project managers. Information must be fully-received with as little interference as possible for it to be effective. Second, project managers must realize how quickly project management information can become complex due to the exponential increase in channels and the increased risk of missing vital information in time. Third, understanding the information is still important even if the information is transmitted clearly and timely. That is because risk management is a comprehensive part of good project management communication. Merely telling someone of risk is not useful if the person does not understand the full impact and probability of the risk event. That is why storytelling should be part of risk management.

Lessons Learned for the Project Manager

• For understanding to occur, the communication must be clear. Therefore, the information transfer communication model complements the emergence communication model.

• Communication complexity can rapidly increase even with a few project team members and stakeholders.

• Project managers need to develop effective ways to manage communication to ensure that information flows freely and to where the information can do the most benefit.

• Project managers are the information hubs of their projects. It is most important that they have effective and efficient ways to receive and transmit project information.

• Project risk management is another form of project communication management.

• Storytelling is an effective tool for project risk management.

CHAPTER SIX - NOISE IN THE CHANNEL? THE IMPORTANCE OF CULTURAL AND EMOTIONAL INTELLIGENCE

In my project management communication research, I found several research articles on the effect of culture on project management communication. I noticed how researchers viewed culture's role in communication. Let me summarize three articles to demonstrate how attitudes toward culture changed in project management communication.

The first article by Loosemore and Lee was published in 2002. The conclusion was that culture was another example of "noise" in the channel which prevents clear communication. The authors' advice was to minimize culture's influence in project communications.

The second article by Stahl et al. (2010) was a study on how culture affected project management communication. This article concluded that, in contrast to the first article, that cultural differences had no direct effect on project management communication. So, we went from cultural differences being noise to not being a barrier, and something project managers can ignore when communicating.

The third article, published by Bohm over ten years later after the first article, explained why project managers needed to consider cultural differences when communicating with project teams and stakeholders. The change in attitudes toward culture exemplifies the contrast between the information transfer model of communication and the emergent model of communication. This shift in attitude is vital as we explore the role of culture in promoting understanding.

From "Noise" to a "Need" in Project Management Communication

"Culture refers to a society's shared values, beliefs, traditions, understandings, assumptions and goals that are learned from previous generations and passed to future generations. . . . Thus communication and culture are inseparable concepts because culture is both learned and maintained through human interaction. Culture not only determines who talks to who, about what and how the communication proceeds, but it also determines how people encode messages, the mediums they chose to transmit them and the way that the symbols (both verbal and non-verbal) contained in the message are interpreted. Since culture is the foundation of communication, it can represent a major source of "noise" which can interrupt or distort the meanings intended in a message. Problems can arise when receivers attribute meaning to a message according to their own cultural frame of reference which can, in some circumstances, be very different to the intentions of the sender. The more different the communicating cultures, the greater the problem. (p. 318)"[xvii]

"Creating a deeper understanding and interest for cross-cultural issues may further improve the effectiveness of project management practices [citing Narayanaswamy and Henry, 2005]. Ignoring differences in teams and organizations may inhibit information systems' implementations in global settings and increase the risk of project failure [citing Harris and Davison, 2002]" (p. 116).[xviii]

Intercultural Communication

In my project management communication course, I have a section on intercultural communication. Intercultural communication is especially important as many of my engineering students come from diverse backgrounds. In my classes of 75 to 100 students, I have had students from Africa, the Middle East, and Asia along with students from all around the U.S., Canada, and South America. I have also had students that are traditional undergraduates and older students returning to school for a second career. If I didn't recognize the cultural differences of my students, my teaching would be ineffective.

In the section on intercultural communication, I introduce the students to Hofstede's Cultural Dimensions. In his model, Hofstede describes six ways that cultures differ from each other:

1. Individualistic to Collectivistic – How personal needs and goals

are prioritized versus the needs and goals of the group/clan/organization.

2. Masculine to Feminine – Masculine societies have different rules for men and women, less so in feminine cultures.

3. Uncertainty Avoidance – How comfortable are people with changing the way they work or live (low UA) or prefer the known systems (high UA).

4. Power Distance – The degree people are comfortable with influencing upwards — acceptance of inequality in distributing power in society.

5. Time Perspective – Long-term perspective, planning for future, perseverance values versus short-time past and present-oriented.

6. Indulgence to Restraint – Allowing gratification of basic drives related to enjoying life and having fun versus regulating it through strict social norms.

In my work at the U.S. Patent and Trademark Office (USPTO), I see these cultural differences in the USPTO's 13,000+ workforce. As I develop and deliver project management training and my other courses, I need to remember how cultural differences can affect how the learners will receive the training. To help me in navigating cultural differences, I use the *Cultural Intelligence* model. Cultural Intelligence (CQ) comprises four parts:

CQ Drive – Your level of interest, persistence, and confidence during multicultural interactions.

CQ Knowledge – Your understanding of how cultures are similar and different.

CQ Strategy – Your awareness and ability to plan for multicultural interactions.

CQ Action – Your ability to adapt when relating and working in multicultural contexts.

Let me give you a simple example of CQ in action. As a young IT project manager, I often mistakenly scheduled meetings during Jewish and Muslim holidays. Coming from a small Kentucky town, I was surrounded by various Christian denominations. It seemed like Winchester had a church on every street corner. However, I can count the number of times on both hands when I encountered a Jewish person. The first Muslim person I encountered was in my first year at college. I just never had to know anything else other than Christian holidays.

So, after two project team members approached me with their concerns, I included Jewish and Muslim holidays on my Outlook calendar so I wouldn't make the same mistake of scheduling during a religious holiday. Today, I have all the major religions' holidays on my calendar.

Now, you may be thinking, how do you keep up with all the cultural differences? We discuss this in my courses and training. As the learners have taught me, the best way to deal with cultural differences is to have an attitude of willingness to learn and patience. Most members of a culture recognize that someone outside of their culture will not know all the cultural practices. But, keeping an open mind and willingness to admit your cultural ignorance is key. Members of a culture are proud of their traditions and welcome the chance to explain their culture to others.

Cultures are not just tied to race, national origin gender, and similar differences among us. Each profession and organization has their own culture. Working in the federal government has taught me that the federal agencies and even the smaller divisions have different cultures. The National Oceanic and Atmospheric Administration (NOAA) has a different culture from the USPTO which is different from the Census Bureau even though we both are under the Department of Commerce (and headquarters has a much different culture from its bureaus).

Each profession also has a culture. A classroom exercise is to ask my engineering students if they have a different culture from English majors. How about the differences between engineering students and math majors? Are engineering students that much different from business majors and how? We then talk about subculture among the engineering students. The electrical engineers from mechanical engineers. The civil engineers from the fire protection students.

In our organizations, we can see the cultural differences in the professions. The lawyers from the finance people. The human resources (HR) people from the information technology (IT) folks. The facilities people from the records manager. As we discussed earlier in the book, people are members of several cultures (social worlds) simultaneously. Each culture/social world has its language and concepts that can change depending on which social world the person is inhabiting now.

The Cultures of Project Teams

What about project teams? Do they have cultures? Absolutely! A famous example is Kelly Johnson's Skunk Works which produced groundbreaking aircraft for the U.S. including the U2 spy plane and stealth technology. Here are Johnson's famous 14 rules for Skunk Works projects:

1. The Skunk Works® manager must be delegated practically complete control of his program in all aspects. He should report to a division president or higher.

2. Strong but small project offices must be provided both by the military and industry.

3. The number of people having any connection with the project must be restricted in an almost vicious manner. Use a small number of good people (10% to 25% compared to the so-called normal systems).

4. A very simple drawing and drawing release system with great flexibility for making changes must be provided.

5. There must be a minimum number of reports required, but important work must be recorded thoroughly.

6. There must be a monthly cost review covering not only what has been spent and committed but also projected costs to the

conclusion of the program.

7. The contractor must be delegated and must assume more than normal responsibility to get good vendor bids for subcontract on the project. Commercial bid procedures are very often better than military ones.

8. The inspection system as currently used by the Skunk Works, which has been approved by both the Air Force and Navy, meets the intent of existing military requirements and should be used on new projects. Push more basic inspection responsibility back to subcontractors and vendors. Don't duplicate so much inspection.

9. The contractor must be delegated the authority to test his final product in flight. He can and must test it in the initial stages. If he doesn't, he rapidly loses his competency to design other vehicles.

10. The specifications applying to the hardware must be agreed to well in advance of contracting. The Skunk Works practice of having a specification section stating clearly which important military specification items will not knowingly be complied with and reasons therefore is highly recommended.

11. Funding a program must be timely so that the contractor doesn't have to keep running to the bank to support government projects.

12. There must be mutual trust between the military project organization and the contractor, the very close cooperation and liaison on a day-to-day basis. This cuts down misunderstanding and correspondence to an absolute minimum.

13. Access by outsiders to the project and its personnel must be strictly controlled by appropriate security measures.

14. Because only a few people will be used in engineering and most other areas, ways must be provided to reward good performance by pay not based on the number of personnel supervised.[xix]

As you read the rules, look between technical project requirements to see the cultural practices. A great example is rule 12 in which Kelly directly addresses the communication practices of the Skunk Works culture. You have two very different organizations, the military, and the contracting firm, developing shared communication practices to increase trust and cut down on issues arising from miscommunication.

Emotional Intelligence

We turn now from examining cultural intelligence to emotional intelligence. Considering emotional intelligence with cultural intelligence is necessary because people are more than just their culture. People are greatly influenced by their cultures, but there are individual ways of perceiving the world that makes each person unique. Recognizing the perspectives of individuals is where a good understanding of emotional intelligence can help the project manager.

Emotional intelligence (EI), first popularized in the 1990s by Daniel Goleman, has become a hot topic in the project management world. You can find numerous books, articles, and courses on emotional intelligence in project management. No need to reproduce the vast information on EI here but I want to demonstrate how EI influences communication.

As discussed earlier in the book, successful persuasive communication rests upon the Aristotle triad of logos, ethos, and pathos. Much of project management communication is heavy on the logos side of communication as we discuss project tasks, schedule, resources, and scope of the project product. However, being aware of our emotions and the emotions of our project team and stakeholders makes project communications effective which helps project success.

The EI model I am certified in is the EQ-i$^{2.0}$ model creating by Multi-Health Systems, Inc. There are five major areas to the EQ-i$^{2.0}$ model:

Self-Perception – how the regards themselves, how self-actualized the person is, and the level of awareness of their own emotions.

Self-Expression – The assertiveness and the independence of the person along with how they express their emotions.

Interpersonal – The number and type of interpersonal relationships a person has along with the person's sense of social responsibility and empathy.

Decision Making – How well the person controls their impulse, their reality testing ability which aids in problem-solving.

Stress Management – Probably most relevant to project managers is the concepts of flexibility, stress tolerance, and level of optimism.

You are probably familiar with how stress affects you and your project team's ability to communicate effectively. If you have something weighing on your mind, you can't focus enough to create understanding — the same for your project team members and stakeholders. Also, the inability to project the appropriate empathy or even emotional awareness can limit your persuasive abilities.

Using myself as an example, my levels of emotional self-awareness and empathy are low. It doesn't mean I don't have emotions. The low levels mean I ignore emotions in favor of being rational. Ignoring emotions makes sense because in my careers as a paralegal and then IT project manager, I have a good ability to deal with crises. In Boy Scouts, I taught First Aid and wilderness survival skills to other scouts. It was imperative I didn't let my emotions or other people's emotions overwhelm me as I dealt with the emergency. However, strengths taken too far can be a weakness which is why I have increased my emotional intelligence skills. Practicing emotional intelligence skills have helped me become a more effective communicator. Understanding your emotional intelligence levels will help you too as you communicate with your project team and stakeholders.

Ethos is Based on Good EI and CQ

The project manager with good emotional intelligence and cultural intelligence (EI/CI) will be perceived as having a high ethos. Team members will see the high emotional intelligence and cultural intelligence even in the project manager's nonverbal communication. Recognizing emotions in others is because of a special set of neurons in our brains called *mirror neurons*. Mirror neurons help us feel what other people are feeling by simulating the emotions of others as we interact with people. Being more aware of our feelings and other people's feelings help enhance our connection to others and make us more credible.

High emotional intelligence and cultural intelligence also gives a better ability to craft emotionally-compelling communication. Project managers with high EI/CI can use pathos more effectively and make the logos portion of his or her communication more effective. A good balance of ethos, pathos, and logos makes the project manager more persuasive.

High EI/CI also aids creating understanding in project management communications. A project manager with high EI/CI is more in adept at feedback and thus the project manager can test if the recipient of his or her communication has the requisite know-what, know-how, and know-why understanding of the intended messages.

Lessons Learned for the Project Manager

• Understanding cultural differences and emotions will help the project manager be a better communicator by increasing the audience's perception of the project manager's ethos.

Cultural intelligence (CQ) comprises four steps:

CQ Drive – Your level of interest, persistence, and confidence during multicultural interactions.

CQ Knowledge – Your understanding of how cultures are similar and different.

CQ Strategy – Your awareness and ability to plan for multicultural interactions.

CQ Action – Your ability to adapt when relating and working in multicultural contexts.

• Cultures are not only based on race, national origin, religion, and other ways that make people diverse. Cultures can also be based on a profession, the organization where a person works. Even projects can have their own cultures.

• There are five components of emotional intelligence (EI):

Self-Perception – how the regards themselves, how self-actualized the person is, and the level of awareness of their own emotions.

Self-Expression – The assertiveness and the independence of the person along with how they express their emotions.

Interpersonal – The number and type of interpersonal relationships a person has along with the person's sense of social responsibility and empathy.

Decision Making – How well the person controls their impulse, their reality testing ability which aids in problem-solving.

Stress Management – Probably most relevant to project managers is the concepts of flexibility, stress tolerance, and level of optimism.

• Project managers can increase their levels of CQ and EI through training and practice.

CHAPTER SEVEN - COGNITIVE BIASES AND HOW TO PERSUADE AND NEGOTIATE TO THE WHOLE PERSON

According to my students, one of the most memorable class exercises is when I have them go to Wikipedia and examine the list of cognitive biases[xx]. As the students are reviewing the list, I explain that cognitive biases cause errors in how we perceive information or reason with information. I then divide the students into groups and have the groups choose two or three cognitive biases to discuss with the rest of the class.

Each group must answer three questions: what is the bias? How does the bias affect our ability to reason? How do you communicate effectively with someone who has that bias? It's fascinating to watch as each group first marvels at the number of biases and then struggles to find strategies to deal with a person who has that specific cognitive bias.

Let me give an example. Let's say you are in one group which chooses the IKEA effect. According to Wikipedia, the IKEA effect is when a person places greater weight on what they personally created over other items not created by that person. The name comes from psychological experiments in which people who built figures out of LEGO blocks were more likely to ask for more money to part with the figure than if the person was handed a fully-built figure and then asked to sell the figure.

You may have seen the IKEA Effect when working with someone with a new idea for a project management tool or method. If you are discussing a set of project management tools to work with for a project, the person may continually advocate for his or her created tool even if it isn't the best tool for that project. Thus, your group's charge is to determine how to persuade the person to give equal weight to all the project management tools when considering which project management tool to use.

Cognitive biases differ from logical fallacies. Logical fallacies occur when we make mistakes in reasoning. Remember the classic syllogism:

All men are mortal.

Socrates is a man.

Therefore, Socrates is mortal.

If we instead say that:

All men are mortal.

Socrates is a man.

Therefore all men are Socrates.

We have made an error in logic. Logical fallacies result from errors in our System 2 type of thinking.

Cognitive biases are different in that the error arises from how we remember something, what we pay attention to, or the way we treat a piece of information. Cognitive biases usually happen in the way we use System 1 heuristics ("rules of thumb") as we react to the world. As explained in an earlier chapter, System 1 thinking is mostly unconscious and immediate while System 2 is conscious and requires much mental energy. Seeing a dark shadow out of the corner of our eye and quickly reacting to perceived danger is an example of System 1 thinking. Working our way through a list of project risks and applying probability and impact estimates is System 2 thinking.

Heuristics are not inherently bad or flawed. Good heuristics can save time and mental energy. Most heuristics started as deliberative and well-constructed System 2 methods that, after time and validation by constant use, became a System 1 heuristic. For example, what separates a novice chess player from a grandmaster is the number of chess patterns that the grand master has stored in his or her memory. Brain scans of a novice chess player show much more brain activity as the novice's System 2 thinking kicks into overdrive considering all possible chess moves. The chess grandmaster's brain is comparatively less active as he or she only needs to retrieve the appropriate heuristic and follow its instructions.

A problem with cognitive biases is that the cognitive bias short-circuits understanding by presenting the illusion of understanding. For example, let's say an executive sponsor has a recency bias. That is the cognitive bias of being persuaded by the latest information that the person hears no matter the relevance or weight of the new information. Consider this possible scenario:

You are briefing the executive sponsor on the latest project status. You have a list of three risk events arranged from the highest probability of occurring and the most impactful. The first risk event is almost sure to happen and will delay the project for six months. The second risk event has about a 50-50 chance of occurring and will delay the project no more than two months. The third risk event is, at most, at 25% of occurring and will delay the project no more than a week. After you present the risk events, the executive sponsor is fixated on the third event, and you spend the rest of the meeting discussing how to handle what is the least important of the risk events. Just because it was presented last.

For my students, the strategy is simple: switch the order in which you present the risk events. My next question is how do the students know what the cognitive bias is when meeting with a stakeholder for the first time? Do we memorize the list of cognitive biases? Or maybe assign the list to a project team member to silently scan the list while the stakeholder speaks and check off the suspected cognitive biases? Essentially, how do we test for understanding as we interact with the stakeholder or stakeholders? Determining the cognitive bias leads to a discussion of using feedback to test how the stakeholder is processing and understanding the information you are giving.

Cognitive Bias Mitigation are a set of strategies that can help us make better decisions. Consider the following checklist derived from a *Harvard Business Review* article by Daniel Kahneman, Dan Lovallo, and Olivier Sibony.[xxi] As you go through the list, you can see how the cognitive biases can impede your decision-making processes. Also, the checklist demonstrates how different cognitive biases can work together to produce bad decisions by hindering communication.

The Decision Quality Control Checklist

1. "Is there any reason to suspect the team making the recommendation of errors motivated by self-interest?" [Self-Interested Biases]

2. "Has the team fallen in love with its proposal?" [Affect Heuristic]

3. "Were there dissenting opinions within the team? Were they explored adequately?" [Groupthink]

4. "Could the diagnosis be overly influenced by an analogy to a memorable success?" [Saliency Bias]

5. "Are credible alternatives included along with the recommendation?" [Confirmation Bias]

6. "If you had to make this decision again in a year's time, what information would you want, and can you get more of it now?" [Availability Bias]

7. "Do you know where the numbers came from? Can there be . . . unsubstantiated numbers?. . extrapolation from history? . . . a motivation to use a certain anchor?" [Anchoring Bias]

8. "Is the team assuming that a person, organization, or approach that is successful in one area will be just as successful in another?" [Halo Effect]

9. "Are the recommenders overly attached to a history of post decisions?" [Sunk-Cost Fallacy and Endowment Effect]

10. "Is the base case overly optimistic?" [Overconfidence, Planning Fallacy, Optimistic Biases, and Competitor Neglect]

11. "Is the worst case bad enough?" [Disaster Neglect]

12. "Is the recommending team overly cautious?" [Loss Aversion]

How Cognitive Biases Lead to Organizational Failure

Back in 2004, I was working on my Ph.D. in Public Policy and Management. My focus was on government leadership and especially how leaders could produce failure in government projects. As I studied the notable government project failures, I noticed a pattern or framework emerging. I called this my general framework for project failure. My model is over a decade old, but I still see it in the latest project failures (or in general large-scale organizational failures).

Organizational Failure Analysis Framework in Detail

The general model of how failure occurs in organizations has three levels - leadership, team, and organization. Surrounding the three levels are the organization's culture, communication methods, and accountability processes. Each level helps to generate latent conditions individually or with the other layers and thus the conditions for a failure to occur build up over time. Each level also can generate the active failure that, with the latent conditions, causes the eventual major failure.

Before going further, a quick note on how failure occurs in an organization. *Latent conditions* are not failures in of themselves but set up the conditions for failure. Think of latent conditions as freezing weather causing black ice to build upon the surface of a road. The black ice is a latent condition that makes an *active failure* – a car crash – more likely to occur.

Level One – Bad Leadership and Idea Imposition Process

The first level, leadership, generates latent conditions through the interaction of the leader's or leaders' cognitive biases which lead to a bad decision. The noted researcher in decision making, Paul Nutt

(2002), observes that over half of all decisions fail and that two out of every three decisions use bad decision processes.

The steps for ideal decision making are:

1. Formulation of goals

2. Formulation of models and gathering of information

3. Prediction and extrapolation

4. Planning of actions, decision making, and executions of actions

5. Review of effects of actions and revision of strategy[xxii]

But, decision makers often fail to follow these steps for several rules for several reasons. They act without analysis, fail to anticipate side-effects and the long-term outcomes, and assume that the if nothing bad immediately happens then their decision must have been right. Decision makers also are blind to potential changes in the situation.

Formulation of goals is the first step in decision making. Failure in this stage essentially dooms the rest of the decision-making process. In complex situations, decision makers are tempted to achieve multiple goals. Pursuing multiple goals increases the complexity because there will be interrelationships between the goals that may hide negative effects. Think of the analogy of how drugs can sometimes interact to produce harmful effects.

After the goals have been formulated, the decision maker then collects information and analyzes the problem to generate alternatives. Nutt advises that the decision maker should engage in a *discovery process* where they objectively study the situation and the facts surrounding it. There are four phases to the discovery process:

1. Analyzing the problem

2. Exploring various options

3. Selection of an option

4. Monitoring the consequences of the option.

In failed decisions, the decision maker engages in an "idea-imposition process." The decision maker concludes first and then search for supporting evidence. In the idea-imposition process, the search is limited, few ideas are examined, and the effects rarely are monitored. The idea-imposition process is where you can see the effects of cognitive biases interacting with each other.

Level Two – Damaging the Work Teams through Deindividuation and Groupthink

The second level, *Team*, will often respond to pressure from the first level by engaging in groupthink and thus either risky shift or avoidance will occur creating more latent conditions. The rivalry between other teams on this level will also encourage groupthink as teams compete for the attention of the leadership on the first level.

Irving Janis was the first researcher to study groupthink in his book 1972 book, *Victims of Groupthink*. He argued that many disastrous decisions made in American foreign policy were due to the suppression of dissenting or contradictory views during the decision-making process. He found that groups prone to groupthink have these eight symptoms:

1. Excessive optimism about their abilities which encourages taking great risks.

2. The belief that the group is more moral than anyone outside of the group.

3. Ignoring any information that challenges assumptions made by the group.

4. Stereotyping outsiders as weak, stupid, or evil.

5. Self-censoring any threatening ideas.

6. The assumption that all group members agree.

7. Pressuring group members to stay in line with the group consensus.

8. Group members who keep contrary information or opinions out of the decision-making process.

According to Janis, groups must have these pre-existing conditions before becoming susceptible to groupthink. The first condition is that the group must have high cohesiveness in that group members avoid disagreements in favor of group harmony. The second condition is related to how insulated the group is and how powerful the leader is. Groups isolated from outside influences and subject to a leader who controls all discussion is more likely to fall victim to groupthink. Related to the first two conditions is the third condition in which the group feels threatened by external threats. As you can see, these three conditions work together to drive the group members to depend on each other and ignore the outside world.

During my research on the general failure model, I discovered Dr. Paul 't Hart's work on groupthink. Dr. Hart observes there seems to be a paradox in Janis' groupthink regarding the antecedent condition of high group cohesiveness. Under Janis' theory, group members either censor themselves or are pressured by other group members and the group leaders to stifle dissent and support the decision. But Hart counters it is more likely that a tightly-knit group would make better decisions in his examination of group decision making. Hart also argues that cohesiveness is unnecessary for groupthink because *anticipatory compliance* (giving in before the decision maker can exert pressure) can substitute for high cohesiveness.

Along with anticipatory compliance, Hart also adds the concept of *deindividuation* to groupthink theory. Deindividuation results in the team member:

1. Having difficulty in monitoring his or her behavior along with the behavior of the other team members

2. Losing his or her sense of ethics

3. Losing his or her ability to self-correct his or her behavior

4. Experiencing a lack of foresight

5. Developing a lack of concern over future punishment.

Eventually, deindividuation lowers the team member's ability to protest the decision based on personal ethics. The group becomes the team member's main point of reference for morality.

Another concept that Hart adds to groupthink theory is *entrapment*. Entrapment is closely related to the sunk-cost fallacy in which team members continue to commit to a failing course of action hoping to recoup their earlier losses based on the course of action. Entrapment will lead teams to make more risky decisions – *risky shift*. Cognitive biases can also increase the effects of the risky shift.

Level Three – Organization

The third level, organization, is the level where hazards are prevented from harming the organization's assets by a series of defenses (technical, policy, and administrative). The latent conditions flowing from the first two levels erode the defenses in several ways:

1. Rules and safety procedures may be ignored by decisions from either the team or leadership levels.

2. The first two levels may emphasize production over protection, and thus the defenses are underfunded and lack resources.

3. Or, the first two levels may over overemphasize protection and increase the complexity of the defenses to the point they are unworkable and may even encourage further rule breaking.

4. The organization increasingly uses temporary fixes to handle near-failures. Over time, these temporary fixes may become permanent and thus generate unforeseen latent conditions of their own.

As latent conditions continue to build and erode the defenses, the chance for an active failure to breach all the defenses grows.

Culture, Communication, and Accountability

Culture, communication, and accountability transmit and enable the effects of latent conditions. Culture determines the relationships between the three levels but is especially significant with the first two. A culture that encourages leaders to make quick decisions without examining their biases and then impose these decisions onto demoralized teams will produce a greater number of latent conditions than a culture where leaders are encouraged to reflect on their decisions, and teams feel secure enough to question decisions openly.

Communication is also vital because it is how culture is transmitted along with how the decisions from the first level are perceived and transmitted to other levels. You can see why understanding is a vital part of communication.

Accountability's role is that of determining the quality of decisions. If a decision maker knows that they will be held specifically accountable for the results of their decision, they are more likely to care in crafting that decision for the good of the organization. Otherwise, the decision maker may decide for their gain without regard to the damage it may cause the organization.

Good culture, communication, and accountability minimize the number of latent conditions which decreases the probability of an active failure. Bad culture, communication, and accountability can greatly increase the number and severity of latent conditions which increases the probability of an active failure.

Lessons Learned for the Project Manager

• Cognitive biases are erroneous ways we receive and/or process information.

• Cognitive biases can arise from the heuristics (*rules of thumb*) that we have created in System 2 thinking which have become reasoning shortcuts we use in System 1 thinking.

• Use the Decision Quality Checklist to warn you of the common cognitive biases that can affect your decision-making.

• Cognitive biases can lead to larger organizational failure by causing leaders to adopt the idea-imposition process.

• The idea-imposition process can harm project teams by causing deindividuation among the team members. Deindividuation is a form of a group think which causes teams to take greater risks and fail to question decisions.

• Failure to question decisions and take unnecessary risks will increase the number of latent conditions thus growing the chance of organizational (or project) failure.

CHAPTER EIGHT - OUT OF SIGHT BUT STILL IN MIND: VIRTUAL PRESENCE

As our project work becomes more virtual and digitized, project managers are now managing project teams and dealing with stakeholders online and who work remotely. If 90% of a project manager's job is communication, easily more than half of the communication (at least) is through email, phone, texting, and other digital methods. And I am certain that you, as a project manager, have had some training on using Microsoft Project or similar project management software. I can also say with some certainty you have prepared at least one PowerPoint project briefing in your career.

However, with the number of communication tools at our disposal, why isn't our communication any better? How often have you or someone you know misinterpreted an email? Have you been distracted during an online video meeting? Misunderstood a text message? Are you bored to a stupor by a PowerPoint presentation?

John Medina, the author of *Brain Rules*[xxiii], writes that our brains were designed for face-to-face communication and is only fully-engaged when we are in personal contact with each other. As he states, we "ought to really understand that the brain processes meaning before it processes detail. It wants the meaning of what it is that you're talking about before it wants the detail of what it is you're talking about."[xxiv] Think about the most recent briefing you sat through. Were you bored and frustrated because the speaker pummeled you with details while your brain was trying to understand the big picture behind the details?

Five Reasons Why Virtual Communication Is Hard

Nick Morgan, author of *Can You Hear Me? How to Connect with People in a Virtual World* (2018), argues there are five reasons why virtual communication is difficult:

The first reason is lack of feedback. Our brains are constantly searching for signs of danger and making predictions based on what our senses are telling us. We notice many details when speaking face-to-face with a person. How his or her voice sounds, how the person smells, how close the person is, how the person holds themselves, and so on. All these details, mostly processed by our unconscious mind, alert us to possible danger. In other words, we want to know why first and then how or what.

In the virtual world, we lack these details. So, our minds fill in the missing information with best guesses. Have you read an email from someone you know, and, in your head, you hear the email in that person's voice? Have you been puzzled by someone's expression during a video conference to only to discover later that the person was not reacting to you but something off-camera? When deprived of the usual sensory cues, your mind works overtime to fill in the missing details of the communication.

The second reason is lack of empathy. As discussed in an earlier chapter, people relate to each other emotionally through mirror neurons. We use the mirror neurons to help us understand each other's emotions and thus increase our understanding of the message from the person. Take away the empathy, and you are left guessing the emotional impact of a message. The lack of emotional cues is why sarcasm doesn't work well in email or texts.

Not controlling your persona in the digital world is the third reason. In the digital world, all communications are recorded and remembered. Every misstatement, bad joke, unflattering photo, and communication mistake is forever memorialized and accessible. The lack of control has a chilling effect on virtual communication.

The fourth reason, the lack of emotion is closely tied to the lack of empathy. Virtual communications strip away emotions which some might think is the preferred alternative. How often have you heard that emotions prevent us from making good decisions?

Research with people who have damaged emotional centers in their brains has shown that being purely rational makes for bad decision making. Emotions help us prioritize what is important and helps us choose between alternatives. People without emotions cannot make decisions because most alternatives look equally valid to the person. Put a purely rational person in front of a restaurant menu, and he or she will spend hours determining what to order.

An interesting observation by Mr. Morgan is the value of vocal undertones in relaying emotional information. According to research, people naturally gravitate toward leaders because of the undertones in their voices (among other characteristics). However, those undertones are lost because of signal compression in modern digital communications.

The fifth and final reason that virtual communication is not as effective is the lack of connection. Social networking gives us the illusion of connection. However, how much do you know and trust the people you have connected with on Facebook and LinkedIn? For me, I don't connect on Facebook with anyone I haven't met in real life (with a few exceptions). On LinkedIn, I will connect with anyone that shares my professional interests. However, I feel more like my true self on Facebook than on LinkedIn. But nothing beats real connection than dinner with friends.

These five reasons do overlap and are heavily based on the emotional aspects of communication. Virtual communication demonstrates the triumph of the information transfer model of communication in which we have cleaner and cleaner channels to transmit messages from senders to receivers. So, we can effectively transmit more information at higher speeds. However, we are stripping out the emotional aspects of the communication. And thus, as information transfer model of communication has made the digital world possible, it is contributing to even greater miscommunication.

The Rise of the Long-Distance Leader

Kevin Eikenberry and Wayne Turmel have chronicled the rise of the long-distance leader in their 2018 book, *The Long-Distance Leader: Rules for Remarkable Remote Leadership*. According to their research, most leaders are dealing with teams that either work remotely part of the time or full-time. Interestingly, the number one concern of remote leaders is not that their people are working. Rather, the leaders worry most about leading effectively when the leader is not physically present.

As Eikenberry and Turmel observe, these aspects of leadership are still the same whether the leader is remote or in the next office. First, the leader's focus should be on his or her people. Second, the fundamentals of human behavior are still the same. So is the third aspect which are the principles of leadership. The fourth aspect is that the leader's roles in coaching, mentoring, and influencing are still vital. Finally, being expected to produce results is still an important aspect of the leader's role.

What has changed is that the leader is out-of-sight. Technology filters out both the information being received and the communication cues necessary for understanding. These filters change your working relationships and what your people need to do their work. Leaders and followers will often feel more isolated due to the remoteness. Feelings of remoteness will require the leader to change his or her leadership approach to reestablish a sense of connection with the leader and fellow project team members.

The Remote Leadership Model

To aid remote leaders, Eikenberry and Turmel propose two models for effective remote leadership. The first model, *Remote Leadership Model*, comprises three interlocking areas. First is the *Leadership and Management area* in which leaders develop their "remarkable leadership" skills:

1. Continuous learning

2. Championing change

3. Communicating powerfully

4. Building relationships

5. Developing others

6. Focusing on customers

7. Influencing with impact

8. Thinking and acting innovatively

9. Valuing collaboration and teamwork

10. Solving problems and making decisions

11. Taking responsibility and being accountable

12. Managing project and processes successfully

13. Setting goals and supporting goal achievement

The second area of the model is *Tools and Technology*. Tools and technology are probably where remote leaders struggle the most as the current online tools and technology are not robust enough to fully transmit the nuances of our communications. Effective remote leaders learn how to work around the limitations of the technology to get his or her meaning through.

The third area is *Skill and Impact* which is where the remote leader is continually refining his or her skills in remote leadership. Continuously improving remote leadership skills could involve being up-to-date on the latest communication technology or finding effective methods of reducing isolation among the project manager and the project team members.

The Three O Model of Leadership

Eikenberry and Turmel then offer a second model to assist the remote leader. The *Three O Model of Leadership* compels the remote leader to focus on *outcomes*, *others*, and *ourselves*. Remote work can be challenging due to isolation, lack of environmental cues when communicating with team members, and long silences between messages. These challenges can cause a lack of focus on outcomes and other team members.

Because the remote leader is isolated, it is easy for the remote leader to focus on him-or-herself to the detriment of the project outcomes and the project team members. Remote leaders need to develop cues to make up for the physical cues that would be present if the leader was physically present with his or her team.

So, how does the remote leader communicate effectively to create trust and understanding at a distance? Eikenberry and Turmel's present the *Trust Triangle* in chapter eleven of their book. To build trust, you and your team must agree on a common purpose. Then, there must be an alignment of motives along with the competence of you and your team to fulfill the project. The authors suggest the following for building trust at a distance:

1. Use meetings strategically such as highlighting the great work a person has done. Let people ask each other for help during the meeting. Yes, have an agenda and keep meetings on time. However, build in some time for people to get to know each other as this may be the only time, they interact with each other.

2. Praise people in public.

3. Delegate tasks in public.

4. Let team members get to know each other by mixing up task teams, have team members work together on special projects, or celebrate accomplishments.

5. Use the technologies to the fullest extents. Use webcams. Instant messaging is also good for quick questions.

6. See something, say something. The authors give the example of a leader suddenly being copied on emails sent between two team members. Unusual email traffic may indicate to call each team member up and ask what is going on.

Being remote doesn't mean that the project manager cannot effectively communicate. Remote leaders need to find new ways to work with the distance and technology to help build the trust to create the understanding necessary for effective project management communication. Being a long-distance leader has not changed the fundamentals of human behavior and the principles of leadership. Remote leadership does require that the project manager needs to constantly check that his or her messages are being received and understood despite the limitations caused by distance and technology.

Lessons Learned for the Project Manager

• Most leaders have at least some remote workers either full-time or part-time.

• Communicating with remote project team members is difficult because the online communication technology impedes feedback, emotional connection, and empathy. Because of these impediments, the brain is starved for details needed to create understanding.

• The Remote Leadership Model compels remote leaders to focus on their leadership skills, the tools and technology of online communication, and their skills and impact.

• The Three O Model of Leadership helps remote leaders overcome the effects of isolation by having remote leaders concentrate on achieving outcomes, helping others on the team, and taking care of his-or-herself.

• To build trust with remote workers, the project manager and the project team members must agree on a common purpose while aligning their motives and being transparent in their behaviors.

CHAPTER NINE - THE COACHING, SITUATIONAL, AND SERVANT PROJECT MANAGER

This chapter is the culmination of our journey from understanding the new model of project management communication. This chapter is also a good picture of how project management leadership has evolved. Projects are becoming more complex. The project team has become more diverse and is filled with remote and virtual workers. Increasing demands projects produce not just financial results but, socially beneficial results. The project manager's role has transformed from being the person who maximizes the balance between project resources, the schedule, and tasks to deliver a project on time, within budget, and meets the expectations of the customer. The project manager is more than just a traditional manager; the project manager must become a leader.

In my leadership development courses, I work with leaders throughout government to understand how to use situational leadership, servant leadership, and coaching leadership to better their leadership abilities. In the next sections, I will explain briefly how each leadership model works and the role of communication in each leadership model.

Situational Leadership

The idea behind situational leadership is that the leader uses one of four leadership styles depending on the level of a follower's task ability and motivation. The first leadership style is the "telling" style in which the leader closely works the employee to teach him or her the job. The second leadership style is the "selling" style in which the leader still works closely with the employee but allows the employee to offer suggestions. The leader then moves to the third style, "participatory," in which the employee is given more opportunities to participate in the decision making. The fourth style is "delegating" where the employee is given maximum latitude to make their own decisions about the work.

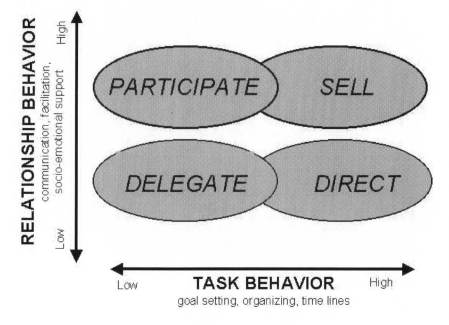

Figure 4: The Four Styles of Situational Leadership

To determine which leadership style to use with an employee, the leader needs to assess the employee's level of task ability and motivation. Most beginning employees are highly-motivated but lack the level of competence in their job. As the employee learns his or her job, he or she may become less motivated as he or she realizes the full complexity of their jobs. As the employee becomes proficient in his or her work, the leader concentrates on increasing the motivation level of the employee. When the employee has reached the appropriate level of motivation and task ability, the leader delegates as much of the work and decision-making to the employee.

Communication is the key to situational leadership. There are six key conversations.

The alignment conversation – the leader and the employee both agree on the leadership style used.

The directive conversation - Have you ever seen someone excited to accomplish a new goal or project yet doesn't have a clue where to start? Leaders need to have directive conversations with those individuals to build their competence and maintain their commitment and enthusiasm. They need their leader to explain the who, what, where, when, and why of the work they're being asked to do, as well as being given the training and resources needed to accomplish their goals. Directive conversations set a firm foundation for an individual's success.

The coaching conversation - Individuals discouraged with their lack of progress or success in achieving a goal need coaching conversations with their leader. Coaching conversations blend high amounts of direction and support to pull individuals out of their disillusionment and help build their competence on the goal or task. The direction looks like continued training, instruction, and assistance in problem-solving. Support from the leader includes listening, praise, and encouragement to help build the individual's commitment and motivation.

The supportive conversation - Leaders engage in supportive conversations with those individuals with the skills and abilities to do the job but lack the confidence to take their work to the next level. Supportive conversations involve heavy doses of listening, asking open-ended questions that allow individuals to solve their problems, and offering the praise and recognition they need to help boost their confidence.

The delegating conversation - Leaders have delegating conversations with individuals who are high performing, self-reliant, motivated, and competent. These people need their leaders to affirm their competence and commitment by giving low amounts of direction and support. Leaders delegate the goal or task to these individuals and let them run with the ball, yet still being available on the sidelines to assist as needed.

The one-on-one conversations - These 15-30-minute conversations, occurring every 1-2 weeks, help leaders stay in touch with their employees' goals and provide them the opportunity to ask for the direction and support they need from their leaders. One on Ones keep the lines of communication open between leaders and direct reports and allow for mid-course corrections if performance gets off-track.

As you can see, the key to effective communication as a situational leader is understanding. A situational leader must be able to develop an understanding of all four stages of situational leadership. Mere information transfer will not work here. A situational leader must be effective in the Aristotle triad of logos, pathos, and ethos to engage and guide employees.

Servant Leadership

In my leadership development training, I use situational leadership as a bridge to servant leadership. As a project manager, I was trained in servant leadership which flips the old model of the command-and-control leader. Instead of using commands and control where the leader is the center of attention, the servant leader guides from behind. The servant leader supports and serves the employees by providing resources and encouragement. Under servant leadership, the employees are given maximum freedom to determine how to accomplish the work based on the leader's vision.

However, the employees of a servant leader must be proficient in their work and highly-motivated to do the work. High levels of trust must exist between the leader and the employees for servant leadership to be effective. There must be effective communication between the servant leader and employees to build trust. And that means building trust requires good communication through understanding.

Coaching Leadership

Complementary to both styles of leadership is the ability of the leader to coach employees. A popular model for coaching is called the GROW Model.

Goal – Work with the employee to set short-term and long-term goals.

Reality – Then, have the employee do a self-assessment to see where he or she stands right now regarding his or her goals.

Options – The leader and employee work together to determine options to reach his or her goals.

Wrap-up – The employee identifies possible barriers to the options and commits to actions to help reach the goals.

The key to good coaching is developing the trust needed to effectively coach employees. The trust is built on effective communication that helps the employees and the leader develop an understanding of each other.

Lessons Learned for the Project Manager

• Situational Leadership, Servant Leadership, and Coaching Leadership all shift the leadership model from command-and-control to develop-and-support.

• Situational Leadership is where leaders develop both the task competence and confidence for increased independence and autonomy.

• Servant Leadership is where the leader spends most of his or her time coaching employees and supporting their work. Employees have the most autonomy and independence under a servant leader.

• Coaching Leadership is a leadership style used in both Situational Leadership and Servant Leadership.

• The common component to all three leadership styles is good communication based on creating understanding between the leader and the team members.

CHAPTER TEN - PRACTICAL STEPS TO BEING A PERSUASIVE PROJECT MANAGER

I hope I have given you a richer perspective of project management communication. As a practicing project manager from IT projects to government training projects, I know the value of good communication. I also know the damage that miscommunication can cause. Let me give you an example:

Early in my career, I worked on a project to convert a set of online applications from a closed technology platform to Internet browser-based applications. I just finished creating a complex application that was met with great approval by the client. Convinced that I was an amazing programmer and project manager, I built a second application based on what I did for the first application.

The second application was for a different office for the client organization. I had one meeting with the new office in which I did most of the talking — pure information transfer on my part. The client told me what they needed. I only listened for what confirmed my opinions. I quickly built the application and sent it to the client.

The next day, I was called into my boss's office. On the speakerphone was an irate client who accused my company of selling them an "over-engineered" and "gold-plated" product. My miscommunication almost had me fired. From that day, I worked hard in – **fully** – understanding the client's needs.

The Big Picture of Project Management Communication

In my project management course, I use a visual syllabus to show how all the semester's topics fit together. It is a road map to what I want the students to achieve in gaining new knowledge, skills, and abilities. Here is the visual syllabus for this book:

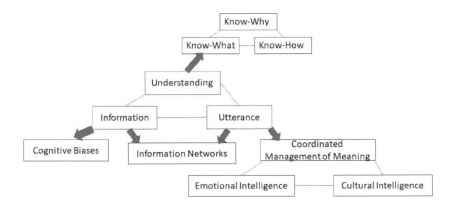

Figure 5: The Book's Visual Syllabus

Building on the emergence communication model of *information*, *utterance*, and *understanding*, you can see how the topics in this book work together. For the information part, the communicator considers the audience's *cognitive biases*. Connecting information and utterance are the concepts around *information networks* such as creating a clear message. Moving to utterance, the communicator builds *coordinated management of meaning* through *emotional intelligence* and *cultural intelligence*. Finally, we move to understanding and the *know-what, know-how*, and *know-why* triangle.

So, how do you use this information in your project management work?

How Do You Make Understanding an Essential Part of Your Project Management Communication?

Understanding starts with yourself. I have worked on my presentation skills, discovered my cognitive biases, and have taken assessments from Myers-Briggs to emotional intelligence. I continually work on upgrading my knowledge and skills by being active in professional organizations and pursuing certifications.

While you are working on yourself, determine what you want to achieve in the communication. All your project management communication should have a strategic goal. Once you have clarified the purpose of your message and what you want to accomplish with your message, you have the necessary information to send.

The next step is to decide on the level of understanding you want to achieve. What is the know-why, know-what, and know-how that your audience will need to understand your message fully? Do you understand the social worlds of your audience and how the audience's perspectives will affect their understanding? What cognitive biases does your audience have?

Then, prepare yourself and your message. Do a self-check on your presentation. Do you have a good balance of ethos, pathos, and logos? Have you built a foundation of trust that will help reach the employees on site with you and the remote workers? Do you have stories that will help make it easier for your audience to process the message?

Have you spent the time building effective communication networks and ways to determine if your audience has clearly received your message? Remember, the more people you need to communicate to, the better your feedback channels and methods for spreading information must be. You need to verify that everyone affected has received the message and fully understood the message.

This is a lot! So, as with any self-improvement program, take it slow and work on a few things at a time. Being a proficient communicator takes time and practice. I learned this from an early age when I had visions of myself as a great debater when I joined the high school speech team. It took over a year of painfully losing every high school debate I competed in to finally understand how to be persuasive. Thanks to persistence and honest reflection, I became a champion college debater.

One more teaching story. A few months after being pulled into the boss's office to hear from the unhappy client, I was sent to another client meeting. The new client needed some work performed on a mobile app. I was called into a board room with five members of the client organization. I briefly introduced myself and then asked the client to tell me their story. For the next twenty minutes, I sat and listened. I occasionally asked a clarifying question but, my focus was on taking good notes. After the client finished, I restated what the client told me so I could check for understanding.

Long story short: the project went well, and I received great praise from the client organization for my good project skills and great communication skills. I find the last comment telling as the client did most of the talking. Communicating for understanding is also knowing when to speak and when to listen.

Thank you for reading this book, and I would love to hear from you. Please send me your comments, suggestions, and criticisms. Also, if these concepts are useful in your project management work, please share so I can include your stories in future editions. I love a good project management teaching story, and I am sure other project managers would benefit from your lessons learned.

REFERENCES

You Are the Message: Getting What You Want by Being Who You Are (2012) by Roger Ailes

If I Understood You, Would I Have This Look on My Face?: My Adventures in the Art and Science of Relating and Communicating (2017) by Alan Alda

Rhetoric (The Complete Three Books) (2011) by Aristotle

Servant Leadership in Action: How You Can Achieve Great Relationships and Results (2018) by Ken Blanchard and Renee Broadwell

Leadership and the One Minute Manager Updated Ed: Increasing Effectiveness Through Situational Leadership II (2013) by Ken Blanchard, Patricia Zigarmi, and Drea Zigarmi

The Long-Distance Leader: Rules for Remarkable Remote Leadership (2018) by Kevin Eikenberry and Wayne Turmel

Conversational Intelligence: How Great Leaders Build Trust and Get Extraordinary Results (2016) by Judith Glaser

Megaproject Management: Lessons on Risk and Project Management from the Big Dig (2013) by Virginia Greiman

The Trust Edge: How Top Leaders Gain Faster Results, Deeper Relationships, and a Stronger Bottom Line (2012) by David Horsager

Thinking, Fast and Slow (2011) by Daniel Kahneman

Leading with Cultural Intelligence: The Real Secret to Success (2015) by David Livermore and Soon Ang

Social Systems (1996) by Niklas Luhmann

Brain Rules (Updated and Expanded): 12 Principles for Surviving and Thriving at Work, Home, and School (2014) by John Medina

Risk Communication: A Mental Models Approach (2001) by M. Granger Morgan, Baruch Fischhoff, Ann Bostrom, and Cynthia Atman

Can You Hear Me?: How to Connect with People in a Virtual World (2018) by Nick Morgan

Making Social Worlds: A Communication Perspective (2007) by W. Barnett Pearce

The Mathematical Theory of Communication (1971) by Claude Shannon and Warren Weaver

CMM Solutions - Field Guide (2012) and *CMM Solutions - Workbook* (2012) by Jesse Sostrin, Barnett Pearce, and Kimberly Pearce

The EQ Edge: Emotional Intelligence and Your Success (2011) by Steven J. Stein and, Howard E. Book

Coaching for Performance: GROWing Human Potential and Purpose - the Principles and Practice of Coaching and Leadership (2010) by John Whitmore

RECOMMENDED BOOKS

Five Stars: The Communication Secrets to Get from Good to Great (2018) by Carmine Gallo

Great explanation of Aristotle's persuasion triad (ethos, pathos, and logos) and how it applies to communication in the information economy. Mr. Gallo has written several books on the speaking secrets of TED Talks that are worth checking out:
- *The Storyteller's Secret: From TED Speakers to Business Legends, Why Some Ideas Catch On and Others Don't* (2016)
- *Talk Like TED: The 9 Public-Speaking Secrets of the World's Top Minds* (2014)

The Fearless Organization: Creating Psychological Safety in the Workplace for Learning, Innovation, and Growth (2018) by Amy C. Edmondson

Gives you a process for creating psychological safety in your organization to help increase engagement and understanding in your workplace.

Project Management Communication Tools (2015) by William Dow and Bruce Taylor

Comprehensive book with many practical templates and tools for managing project communication.

The Power of Communication: Skills to Build Trust, Inspire Loyalty, and Lead Effectively (2012) by Helio Fred Garcia

I've used this as a textbook for several years. Mr. Garcia uses the U.S. Marine Corps' Warfighting to demonstrate how to make your communication strategic and focused.

Team of Teams: New Rules of Engagement for a Complex World (2015) by General Stanley McChrystal, Tantum Collins, David Silverman, and Chris Fussell

How to use communication, transparency, and collaboration to create trust that leads to high-performing teams.

One Mission: How Leaders Build a Team of Teams (2017) by Chris Fussell and C. W. Goodyear

Fussell and Goodyear give the practical steps on creating a team of teams.

Luhmann Explained: From Souls to Systems (2006) by Hans-Georg Moeller

A good introduction to Luhmann's theories on society with a heavy emphasis on communication theory. Not a light read but well worth the effort.

A Mind at Play: How Claude Shannon Invented the Information Age (2017) by Jimmy Soni and Rob Goodman

A good biography of Dr. Shannon and his many accomplishments (including building the first juggling robot).

Destructive Goal Pursuit: The Mt. Everest Disaster (2006 Edition) by D. Kayes

Demonstrates how a single-minded pursuit of goals can destroy teams and destroy a culture of trust. I included it because of the lessons for leaders in being aware of communication problems before the problems get out of hand.

The EQ Leader: Instilling Passion, Creating Shared Goals, and Building Meaningful Organizations through Emotional Intelligence (2017) by Steven J. Stein

Helps the leader learn how to use emotional intelligence to inspire, motivate, and develop their employees while communication with purpose, meaning, and vision.

Cognitive Bias Codex by Design Hacks

Not a book, but a large wall chart that lists all of the identified cognitive biases. I use it in my training to show the sheer number of ways that cognitive biases can affect us.

Communicating Possibilities: A Brief Introduction to the Coordinated Management of Meaning (2017) by Ilene C. Wasserman and Beth Fisher-Yoshida

A good, short overview of how the coordinated management of meaning (CMM) was developed and how it is currently used.

Re-Making Communication at Work (2013) by J. Sostrin

Another good explanation of CMM with a special emphasis on workplace communication.

The Complexity of Human Communication (2012) by Phillip Salem

Dr. Salem describes a complementary model to Luhmann's emergence communication model. Dr. Salem's model goes into detail of how communicators create episodes of communication that create larger stories. Another perspective on CMM.

ABOUT THE AUTHOR

Dr. Bill Brantley has been a project management practitioner and scholar for twenty years. He managed information technology projects as a developer at the Social Security Administration and the U.S. General Services Administration. Bill built web applications for two dot-coms in the early 90s while gaining an MBA in project management and his Professional in Project Management certification. In the mid-90s, Bill decided to obtain his Ph.D. in Public Policy and Management where he focused his studies on project management in government.

While working on his Ph.D., Bill held various board positions with the Kentuckiana Project Management Institute including as president. Between 2003 and 2008, Bill taught online classes in project management to MBA students. In 2008, Bill went back to federal government as an application developer for the U.S. Office of Personnel Management. Since then, Bill has promoted project management in the federal government through his work in the Open Government Movement. In 2012, Bill taught project management communication to engineering students at the University of Maryland. Bill has presented on project management at project management conferences, professional groups, and, recently, the White House Fellows Program.

Bill works at the U.S. Patent and Trademark Office as a trainer and developer in the Enterprise Training Division. Along with his project management certifications, Bill is also a certified professional in training management, a certified professional in learning and performance, and certified data scientist. Please connect with Bill on LinkedIn at https://www.linkedin.com/in/billbrantley/.

If you liked you the book, please leave a review. Or, if you didn't like the book, leave a review anyway. I want to hear from you so I can make the next edition even better.

ENDNOTES

[i] PMI Pulse of the Profession Report 2013 – http://www.pmi.org/-/media/pmi/documents/public/pdf/learning/thought-leadership/pulse/the-essential-role-of-communications.pdf

[ii] Poor Communication Leads to Project Failure One Third of the Time. https://www.coreworx.com/pmi-study-reveals-poor-communication-leads-to-project-failure-one-third-of-the-time/

[iii] Hagen, M., and Park, S. (2013), "Ambiguity acceptance as a function of project management: a new critical success factor," *Project Management Journal* Vol. 44 No. 2, pp. 52–66.

[iv] Koskinen, K. U. (2013), "Observation's role in technically complex project implementation: the social autopoietic system view," *International Journal of Managing Projects in Business* Vol. 6 No. 2, pp. 349–64.

[v] Claude Elwood Shannon is known as the father of information theory for his groundbreaking 1948 article, "A Mathematical Theory of Communication." His innovative insight was to use probability theory to develop a way to measure uncertainty in a transmitted message. "Information entropy" is used to determine the clarity of communication and is the basis for natural language processing used to power Siri and Alexa among other artificial-intelligence voice assistants. Warren Weaver helped popularize Shannon's theory and, in 1949, co-wrote a book with Shannon further popularizing information theory.

[vi] Niklas Luhmann was a German sociologist who wrote 70 books and hundreds of journal articles on systems theory and communication theory. Luhmann's communication theory revolved around understanding and Luhmann spent years exploring how systems could communicate most effectively. Luhmann greatly

influenced German sociology but, his ideas have not been as widely accepted in the U.S. Part of the reason is that Luhmann deliberately wrote his work to be difficult, so readers had to read his work closely.

[vii] **Work Breakdown Structure** (WBS): according to the Project Management Institute, a WBS is a "deliverable oriented hierarchical decomposition of the work to be executed by the project team" A simpler way to define WBS is to think of all the tasks in a project. Now, imagine organizing the tasks into an outline. For example, let's say you are planning a picnic. One set of tasks will be around packing a lunch. Another set of tasks would be packing games for the picnic. And there is an important set of tasks around driving to the picnic spot and setting up the picnic area. A WBS arranges these tasks in the order that a task must be completed before you can work on another task.

[viii] **Monte Carlo Simulation**: To understand Monte Carlo simulations, imagine you are rolling a pair of dice with friends. In this dice game, each of you takes turns rolling the dice to see who rolls the highest sum for each round. To determine how likely it is you will win a round; you can program a spreadsheet to virtually roll the dice a thousand times to create a graph. This graph will show you the probability for each dice sum from 2 to 12. Monte Carlo simulations are often used to determine the probabilities for more complex project risk events.

[ix] Aristotle was one of the three founding fathers of Western philosophy. Along with Socrates and Plato, Aristotle had a profound influence on the Western world's science and culture. Aristotle was the tutor to Alexander the Great, and his writings greatly influenced the medieval world. His contributions to rhetoric still survive after 2,000 years in ethos, pathos, and logos.

[x] *Making Social Worlds: A Communication Perspective*, (2007), pages 100-101.

xi Mihaela, P. A., and Danut, D. (2013), "The measurement and evaluation of the internal communication process in project management," *Annals of Faculty of Economics* Vol. 1 No. 1, pp. 1563–1572.

xii Hagen, M., and Park, S. (2013), "Ambiguity acceptance as a function of project management: a new critical success factor," *Project Management Journal* Vol. 44 No. 2, pp. 52–66.

xiii Bond-Barnard, T. J., Steyn, H., and Fabris-Rotelli, I. (2013), "The impact of a call centre on communication in a programme and its projects," *International Journal of Project Management* Vol. 31, pp. 1006–16.

xiv *Insurance Times: Big Dig is big on safety* by Mark Hollmer, September 17, 2002. https://www.insurancejournal.com/pdf/InsuranceTimes_20020917_38776.pdf

xv Leybourne, S. A., Kanabar, V., & Warburton, R. D. H. (2010). "Understanding and overcoming communications complexity in projects." Paper presented at PMI® Global Congress 2010—North America, Washington, DC. Newtown Square, PA: Project Management Institute. https://www.pmi.org/learning/library/overcoming-communications-complexity-ambiguity-projects-6631

xvi Risk Communication: A Mental Models Approach, 2002, p. 183.

xvii Loosemore, M., and Lee P. (2002), "Communication problem with ethnic minorities in the construction industry," *International Journal of Project Management* Vol. 20, pp. 517–24.

[xviii] Bohm, C. (2013), "Cultural flexibility in ICT projects: a new perspective on managing diversity in project teams," *Global Journal of Flexible Systems Management* Vol. 14 No. 2, pp. 115–22.

[xix] https://www.lockheedmartin.com/en-us/who-we-are/business-areas/aeronautics/skunkworks/kelly-14-rules.html

[xx] https://en.wikipedia.org/wiki/List_of_cognitive_biases

[xxi] *The Big Idea: Before You Make That Big Decision...* by Daniel Kahneman, Dan Lovallo, and Olivier Sibony, June 2011, *Harvard Business Review,* https://hbr.org/2011/06/the-big-idea-before-you-make-that-big-decision

[xxii] Dorner, et al. (1996)

[xxiii] *Brain Rules (Updated and Expanded): 12 Principles for Surviving and Thriving at Work, Home, and School* (Second Edition) (2014) by John Medina.

[xxiv] Quoted in Nick Morgan's *Can You Hear Me?* (2018). Harvard Business Review Press. Kindle Edition.

Made in the USA
Middletown, DE
18 February 2020